Traditional
Chinese Festivals

TRADITIONAL CHINESE FESTIVALS

Marie-Luise Latsch

Graham Brash, Singapore

© *Marie-Luise Latsch, 1985*

First published in 1984 by
New World Press, Beijing

This S.E. Asian edition first published in 1985 by
Graham Brash (Pte) Ltd
36-C Prinsep Street
Singapore 0718

ISBN 9971 947 80 3

All rights reserved

Typeset in 11pt English Times by Superskill Services
Printed in the Republic of Singapore by
Chong Moh Offset Printing Pte. Ltd.

Contents

Foreword ... *7*

China's Traditional Calendar ... *13*

The Spring Festival or the Chinese Lunar New Year ... *24*

The Lantern Festival ... *37*

The Pure Brightness Festival (*Qing Ming*) ... *45*

The Dragon Boat Festival ... *54*

The Mid-Autumn Festival ... *67*

The Kitchen God ... *79*

Chu Xi, the Lunar New Year's Eve ... *86*

Afterword ... *93*

Festivals of the Chinese Minority Nationalities ... *95*

Foreword

My Motivations for Writing this Book

Although traditional festivals are celebrated in many countries throughout the world, China, with its long history and predominantly agricultural society, has a particularly large number of them. A life of agricultural labour is a hard one, and thus festivals have always helped to enliven the daily routine and dispel the weariness of the rural folk, despite the fact that this was not exactly their original meaning. China has still not adopted a Western-style vacation period for its working people. Instead it has stipulated a set number of holidays: on Spring Festival — the Lunar New Year — people in the cities take off three days, while in the countryside the slack period of the agricultural cycle allows peasants even more time; one day on the New Year — according to the Western Gregorian calendar; one day for International Labour Day on May 1; two days starting on Oct. 1 for China's National Day. In addition to these holidays, all city workers enjoy one day off each week.

I lived in Beijing for four years, from 1977 to 1981, working as an ethnologist. During this time I concentrated my research on the significance of the various "traditional" festivals as practised in modern China (referring primarily to the Han nationality areas).

Come the Spring Festival I would frequently be invited to the homes of Chinese friends to celebrate. On other holidays we would enjoy together various specially-made dishes, and my friends would tell tales of how they celebrated these festivals before 1949. As we talked about their childhood memories, I heard also many of the legends concerning the festivals' origins. We find in Western nations as well that the true roots of many important holidays, such as Easter or Christmas, are shrouded in myth and uncertainty.

As I began to compile material and make further inquiries concerning the observance of Chinese traditional festivals, it occurred to me that I might write a book on my findings. Of particular interest to me are the changes in the meaning and practice of the various festivals during the more than 30 years of tremendous change since 1949. In addition, the last several years have seen the revival in rural areas of certain customs that had been taboo during the Cultural Revolution, such as the dragon and lion dances, stiltwalking, and the dragon boat races of Dragon Boat Festival (*Duan Wu Jie*).

The Historical Development of China's Traditional Festivals

The origins of some of China's traditional festivals can be traced as far back as the Shang (C. 1600-1066 B.C.), Zhou (1066-256 B.C.), and Qin (221-207 B.C.) dynasties. Others appeared much later, during the Ming (1368-1644) and Qing (1644-1911) dynasties. In the course of social development, people's customs and habits have undergone gradual changes; some festivals lost their original meaning, taking on new religious content or coming to commemorate historical personages or events (such as Lantern, Pure Brightness — *Qing Ming,* Dragon Boat, and Mid-Autumn festivals).[1]

Some became intertwined with myths, such as Spring Dragon Festival, the Festival of Heavenly Blessings (*Tian Kuang Jie*), the Festival of Reunion (*Qi Xi*), and Chrysanthemum Festival (*Chong Yang Jie*).[2] Some, on the other hand, were for the purpose of worshipping the ancestors and certain deities, or praying for an auspicious future, such as the Festival of Hungry Ghosts, Honouring the Kitchen God (Ji Zao), Lunar New Year's Eve, and Spring Festival.[3]

Besides a number of relatively minor festivals, there have in the past been six major festivals in one year, known in the popular terminology as "Three for the Living", and "Three for the Dead". The former were the Lunar New Year, Dragon Boat Festival, and Mid-Autumn Festival, while the latter grouping consisted of Pure Brightness Festival, the Festival of Hungry Ghosts (also called Feast of All Souls — *Yu Lan Jie*), and *Song Han Yi*, on the 1st day of the tenth month, for sending winter clothes to the ancestors. This last occasion was also referred to as *Shao Yi Jie*, or the Festival for Burning Clothes, in reference to the means of dispatching the clothing to the realm of the ancestors.

In ancient times China's religious festivals were intimately connected with agriculture, from which most of the nation's wealth flowed. A good or bad year influenced not only the material living conditions of the vast majority of the people and the scale of festival observance, but also the very continuation of rule by the emperor and the nobility. At the beginning of spring each year the emperor presided in person over a ceremony in celebration of the beginning of spring ploughing. After offering sacrifices to heaven and earth, he would plough several furrows in a specially prepared plot, thus symbolically marking the start of spring ploughing. In the second month of the lunar calendar came the day for honouring the god of the land. At that time the rulers held ceremonies sacrificing to this deity and also to the ancestors, and prayed for the snow and ice to melt. The third month was the time for the emperor, kings, and various princes and dukes to pray in their ancestral temples for an abundant harvest. With the onset of winter they offered sacrifices in turn to the heaven, earth, and stars in supplication for favourable weather. In the event their prayers were answered, joyous feasts and operatic performances would be held throughout the land.

The common people valued these festivals even more highly. Lunar New Year's Day signals the imminent arrival of spring. During this period there is little to do in the fields, so the peasants have ample time to conduct relatively large-scale festival activities, particularly to beseech the heavens to bestow upon them "harmonious winds and timely rain" in the coming year. With most agricultural activities having been brought to a halt by the onset of winter, people celebrate the abundant harvest just past and hope for a new one to come. Grave Sweeping Festival, which coincides with the spring ploughing, has always been marked by people returning to their family gravesites, putting them in good order, and offering sacrifices to their ancestors. Although Dragon Boat Festival is held to be a day in memory of the poet Qu Yuan, it originally was for worshipping the river deity. Because this was just the time of the summer floods, people feared that incurring the river god's wrath could lead to disastrous floods and the ruination of their crops.

In this book I shall introduce the most important of China's traditional festivals, concentrating on not only their origins and related customs, but also their place in ancient and modern times. Besides the Han people, China has more than 50 other minority nationalities, some of whom have their own indigenous festivals and even their own calendrical system. The present book does not touch on this whole question. In any case it should be pointed out that among the minority nationalities, particularly the Zhuang, most of the Hui, and Manchus, Han festivals have long been very popular. In Japan, Korea and Viet Nam, the Lunar New Year, Lantern Festival, and Mid-Autumn Festival are observed. These festivals are even more treasured by overseas Chinese.

The festivals covered in this book are those which have been most popular both past and present, namely Spring Festival, Lantern Festival, Pure Brightness Festival, Dragon Boat Festival, Mid-Autumn Festival, Honouring the Kitchen God and the Lunar New Year's Eve. I have described the customs and habits by which the broad masses of the people celebrate these festivals, but have omitted all mention of ancient palace ceremonies.

The first chapter is an examination of China's traditional calendar, which turns out to be a rather complicated cross between the familiar Western calendar and the pure lunar system that developed in other parts of the globe. China's traditional festivals are intimately bound up with the agricultural cycle and the changing seasons, as we have seen; thus a basic understanding of the commonly used methods of reckoning time is conducive to a fuller grasp of the significance of the traditional festivals.

---

[1]Lantern Festival falls on the 15th day of the first month of the lunar calendar; Pure Brightness (*Qing Ming*), known in some places as Grave

Sweeping Festival, comes 106 days after the Winter Solstice, on either April 4th or 5th during the early part of the third lunar month; Dragon Boat Festival is on the fifth day of the fifth month; Mid-Autumn Festival on the 15th day of the eighth month.

[2]Spring Dragon Festival is on the second day of the fifth month; the Festival of Heavenly Blessings on the sixth day of the sixth month; the Festival of Reunion, also known as Plea for Dexterity (*Qi Qiao Jie*), on the seventh day of the seventh month; Chrysanthemum Festival on the ninth day of the ninth month.

[3]The Festival of Hungry Ghosts is on the 15th day of the seventh month; Honouring the Kitchen God, the 23rd day of the 12th month in north China, but the 24th day in south China; New Year's Eve is on the last day of the 12th month (either the 29th or 30th); Spring Festival starts on the first day of the first month.

China's Traditional Calendar

In China there are two different calendrical systems in simultaneous use. One is the Gregorian, or Western, calendar, used for official purposes, and the other is the traditional calendar, which is a type of lunar, or more accurately a lunar-solar, calendar. A modern Chinese almanac will include both of these calendars with the dates of the traditional festivals marked on each.

Early Development of the Calendar

In primitive human society, people came to realize that without an ability to accurately foretell seasonal changes it was impossible to sow and harvest the crops and to hunt effectively. Thus, man had to invent the first rudimentary calendar. Long before the invention of scientific astronomical instruments, herdsmen and tillers had for generations observed the position of the moon, sun, planets, and stars, in this way learning how to ascertain the seasons. The earliest instrument of observation was the moon (called "the first measurer" by Bredon and Mitrophanow in their 1927 book *The Moon Year*). Just as the Latin usage indicates — *mensis*, or month, is clearly derived from *mensus*, past participle form of *metici*, to measure — observing the revolutions and phases of the moon was the key to the earliest development of a calendar in the West as well as in ancient China.

It is evident, however, that if farmers wanted to know

when they could plant their crops, a reliance on the moon alone was inadequate. This problem was tackled by observing the stars and planets. Man saw that the relative positions of the stars and the principal planets were not at all haphazard but rather that each one travelled a definite path across the sky. This was followed by the equally important discovery that the waxing and waning of the moon coincide with one group of stars and that the rising and setting of the sun are in harmony with another group. Such knowledge was a great advance in the methods used for determining time-periods and seasons and led directly to the creation of the first lunar and solar calendar.

According to the ancients' rough count, there are about 29½ days from one new moon to the next (we now know the exact number to be 29.5306 days). Therefore 12 revolutions of the moon around the earth require only 354 days, while the earth takes about 365¼ days (365.2422, to be exact) to make one turn around the sun. The solar year, which in actual fact determines the change of the four seasons, can thus have either 12 or 13 full moons. The people of many nationalities in olden times devised different methods to make the lunar year tally with the solar year. Out of their efforts grew the lunar-solar calendar.

The Historical Development of the Chinese Calendar

Regardless of whether a solar or lunar calendar is used, we have seen that there is a gap between the 365.2422 days which the earth actually requires to travel around the sun and the 365 days in a year of the Gregorian calendar, or the

354 days in 12 lunar months. The crucial ingredient to be added that closes the gap is the notion of an intercalary period. In the Gregorian calendar, one day is added every four years (during Leap Year) to realign the calendar year with the actual timespan of the earth's revolution. The extra day is arbitrarily placed at the end of February.

The adjustments to be made in the Chinese lunar calendar are not quite so simple. First of all, some months are assigned 29 days and others 30 (remember that the moon's revolution around the earth takes 29.5306 days). Secondly, an entire intercalary month will be added every two or three years. Each 19-year period will have seven years to which an extra month has been added. In other words, twelve of these years have 12 months each and seven have 13. The question of where precisely in the year the intercalary month is to be inserted is overly technical, but suffice it to say that most often either the fourth or fifth month will be repeated. Thus, the Chinese lunar year once again coincides with the solar year at the end of each 19-year cycle.

The Chinese traditional calendar differs from a purely lunar one, such as that used of old in some Moslem countries, in that it incorporates a yearly cycle of 24 alternating solar and mid-solar terms, each one 15 days long. Each of the four seasons then is subdivided into three solar and three mid-solar terms.

The delineation of the terms is based on the sun's position with regard to the 360 degrees and 12 signs (animal symbols) of the Chinese zodiac. The first day of a given solar or mid-solar term comes when the location of the sun dovetails with the first or 15th degree of one of the zodiac's 12 signs. We can give only an approximate date in terms of the Gregorian calendar for each term, since the 360 degrees of the zodiac diverge from the 365¼ days of the solar year. Thus, we can see clearly why the Chinese traditional calendar must properly be considered a lunar-solar calendar.

Since the duration of one solar and one mid-solar term together is slightly longer than one lunar period, there is sometimes only a single term in one lunar month. The calendar promulgated by the emperor Wu Di of Han dynasty, in the year 104 B.C., stipulated that such a single-term month should be the one to have an intercalary month added. This method of intercalation for China's traditional calendar has been employed right up to the present time.

The yearly cycle of solar and mid-solar terms is closely linked to the changes of nature, so they are extremely useful to the peasants, providing information regarding the proper time for planting and harvesting, for example. Some physically sensitive people are able to discern the imminent arrival of a solar or mid-solar term by means of a bodily response, such as a headache or heightened blood pressure, and other people are simply aware of changed atmospheric pressure or weather conditions.

All of the 24 solar and mid-solar terms are named in accordance with the seasonal changes. The first term is called the Beginning of Spring and falls on the 4th or 5th of February. According to the Xia Calendar (as the traditional calendar is also known), clear weather on that day is a good omen for ploughing. The second term is called Rain Water (on the 19th or 20th of February), when it is hoped there will be no more snow, as the peasants will need rain. On the 5th or 6th of March comes the term known as the Waking of Insects, as the earth awakes from hibernation. In the past, some people held that if thunder sounded then for the first time of the year, the dragon would awake from his winter sleep. On the day of the Spring Equinox (the 20th or 21st of March), people hope for rain, which they believe will bring particular benefit to the crops. Pure Brightness falls on the 4th or 5th of April. If a south wind blows on that day the peasants expect a bumper harvest. Grain Rain which falls on the 20th or 21st of April is the time for peasants to begin sowing the spring wheat. The onset of hot weather comes with the Beginning of Summer on the 5th or 6th of May. The Grain Full occurs on the 21st or 22nd of May. By that time, the winter wheat planted the previous autumn is nearing maturity and will be harvested within a few days. When Grain in Ear comes (on the 5th or 6th of June) all current crops are nearing their limit of growth, and it serves as a deadline for seeding those crops which will be harvested in the fall, such as millet, sorghum, late corn, or beans. A change of weather on this day might be considered an auspicious event. The Summer Solstice (on the 21st or 22nd of June) is the day with the most daylight hours of the whole year. The short period of time following is the most suitable for growing vegetables. The garlic ripens, and as the peasants used to say: "The days around the Summer Solstice are the time for gathering in the garlic." The Slight Heat falls on the 7th or 8th of July and the Great Heat on the 23rd or 24th of the same month. These two terms mark the three ten-day periods of the hottest part of the year. People do not mind the heat, however, because of another old saying which goes "the hotter it is during the dog days of summer, the better quality will the grain be". The Beginning of Autumn comes on the 7th or 8th of August, but the weather remains hot. In fact, the cool weather will not come before the Limit of Heat which falls on the 23rd or 24th of August and represents the true end of summer. In north China, the peasants begin to reap the millet. The dry season begins on the 7th or 8th of September with White Dew when the peasants sow the winter wheat crop. If the sky is covered with white clouds on the Autumnal Equinox, it is believed that the crops planted in late autumn will produce a bumper harvest the following year. In the past, if there were thunder and lightning on this day, it was and probably still is believed that the harvest would be a poor one. When the Cold Dew comes on the 8th or 9th of October, the leaves of trees begin to fall. Frost's Descent on the 23rd or 24th of October marks the earliest appearance of frost. The 7th or 8th of November is the Beginning of Winter, presaging the onset of cold weather. Slight Snow falls on the 22nd or 23rd of November and the Great Snow on the 7th or 8th of December. These are followed in turn by the Winter Solstice of the 22nd or 23rd of December, Slight Cold on the 5th or 6th of January, and Great Cold on the 20th or 21st of January. This brings the cycle of 24 solar and mid-solar terms to an end.

China's traditional calendar was shaped by the development of agricultural production. Legend holds that the Chinese lunar-solar calendar dates from the Xia dynasty (C. 21st-16th century B.C.). It is known variously as the Agricultural Calendar, the Old Calendar, or the Xia Calendar. According to the oracle bone inscriptions of the Shang dynasty (C. 16th-11th century B.C.), an intercalary month had already been adopted by that time. During the Spring and Autumn Period (770-476 B.C.), people were able to mark both the spring and autumn equinoxes and the summer and winter solstices. The delineation of the solar and mid-solar terms was accomplished some time during the Qin (221-206 B.C.) and Han (206 B.C.-220 A.D.) dynasties, and they became the basis of agricultural activities. It must be said, however, that this formulation was based primarily on the climate and farming seasons of north China's Yellow River valley and has never been suitable to conditions in other regions of the country.

The form of the traditional calendar currently in use (the Xia Calendar) which takes the month corresponding to the Gregorian calendar's late January to mid-February as the first month of the year, has not been followed throughout Chinese history. In the Xia dynasty the year began as it does now, but during the Shang (or Yin, as it is also known), the new year began in what is actually the 12th month of the Xia Calendar, and in the Zhou dynasty (1066-256 B.C.) the year started with the 11th month of the present traditional calendar.

The year 104 B.C. — the first year of the Taichu period during the reign of the Han dynasty emperor Wu Di — witnessed a calendar reform, and the Taichu calendar was promulgated. It basically restored the one used in Xia times and proclaimed New Year's Day to be the day of the first new moon after the sun enters the 11th sign of the solar zodiac, known in China as the Dog and in the West as Aquarius. For this reason the new year could not begin earlier than January 21st nor later than February 20th reckoned according to the Gregorian calendar. Wu Di's calendar has continued in use for more than two thousand years with only slight changes during this entire period. When the Republic of China was founded in 1912, the new government officially annulled the old calendar and adopted the Gregorian calendar, to be called the Public Calendar. Since that time the traditional New Year has been called the Spring Festival. But in everyday life the Xia Calendar, deeply rooted in Chinese culture, remains in use along with the new calendar.

Many centuries ago the Imperial Board of Astronomy, which was composed of mathematicians and astronomers, was responsible for compiling a new almanac for each new year and presenting it to the emperor for approval. When the sovereign pronounced it good, a copy would be issued to a high official outside the front gate of the Imperial City — the Gate Which Faces the Sun (*Zheng Yang Men* or *Qian Men*) — and he in turn would forward copies to nobles and other officials throughout the empire. Falsification was punished by death and illegal reprinting of the imperial almanac was an offence against the law.

The Chinese traditional calendar, while conforming to astronomical theory in many respects, was strongly coloured by mystical concepts. The so-called Moon Palaces are the 28 constellations of the lunar zodiac (*Yue Gong* or Moon Palaces Chart), each one identified with a certain animal, by which the path of the moon may be subdivided. The authors of this book drew on both the lunar zodiac and the 12 signs of the solar zodiac to show the connection between celestial phenomena and earthly affairs, thus propagating superstitious ideas to deceive the populace. These astrologers held that virtually all human activities large and small such as sericulture, shopkeeping, shipbuilding, livestock-raising, woodcutting, ditch-digging, building construction, marriages, funerals, travelling, literary work or even bathing and haircutting are affected by changes in the constellations' positions. They made calculations as to which days and hours could be favourable for performing various tasks, or whether the coming harvest would be a good one, or whether one could expect good fortune or bad. Some proverbs still current in the countryside attest to the influence of these beliefs, such as "It is easy to plough the field in the years of the Ox and the Horse". Superstitious sayings of this nature were included in the imperial almanac issued during the Yuan dynasty (1271-1368). Before the founding of the People's Republic of China, all the almanacs in circulation provided this type of information. Even in feudal times, however, there were clear-sighted scholars who opposed the inclusion of such superstitious predictions in the imperial almanac. In the year 1390 during the reign of Ming emperor Hongwu, a minister named Xie Dasheng presented a memorial to the emperor, recommending that only such essential information as the movements of the stars, planets, and moon and the correct time for ploughing, seeding and harvesting be indicated in the almanac. The other types of notations were not only valueless but also superstitious as well, he said, they absolutely did not belong to the imperial almanac.

In 1703, the outstanding Chinese astronomer and mathematician Mei Wending (1633-1721) sternly criticized in one of his works the superstitious predictions that appeared in almanacs. With the approval of the Kangxi emperor (r. 1662-1722), this article of Mei's was included in the imperial almanac as an appendix. He wrote that an almanac should aim to provide information about the seasons and the solar and mid-solar terms for reference particularly to agricultural activities, and that it should not attempt to foretell good fortune or disasters that might befall those on the earth.

Fortune-telling is not, of course, a peculiarity of Chinese almanacs alone. German almanacs published in the 17th and 18th centuries which also appealed primarily to farmers, were richly illustrated with woodcuts and figure paintings.

These exquisite figure paintings can still be seen in an almanac published in the 19th century showing the proper medical treatment for various medical problems, such as how to bleed a patient. Diagrams of the many constellations were further provided to demonstrate in which part of the patient's body medical treatment should be concentrated. There was also a book called the *Centenary Calendar* which was an amalgam of various sorts of superstitious ideas relating to astrology, fatalism, portents, weather forecasting and health care. In German almanacs printed in modern times, we can still see superstitious ideas mixed up together with discussions of the history of calendars and customs.

I would now like to make a brief mention of certain terms used by the Chinese to mark the years. Foremost is the 60-year cycle of year names known as the Heavenly Stems and Earthly Branches (*Tian Gan Di Zhi*). One written character from among the 10 Heavenly Stems is paired with one of the 12 Earthly Branches in a specific fashion, producing a total of 60 code names for as many years. One such cycle is called a *Jia Zi*, based on the names of the first stem and the first branch.

According to Sima Qian (145-87 B.C.), the great historian of the Western Han dynasty, this system first came into use during the Gonghe (841-828 B.C.) period of the Western Zhou dynasty. But the origins of the symbolism involved were not known even in Sima Qian's time, and now the circumstances around the development of these concepts are even less certain. Possibly, however, the choice of 12 Earthly Branches had to do with 12 revolutions of the moon in a year. We can see also that the number 12 corresponds to the number of signs in the solar zodiac.

In addition to the function of the solar zodiac discussed

earlier in the chapter as it related to the solar and mid-solar terms, each of the 12 animal symbols has the further function of identifying a particular year (in a cycle of twelve years). Almost every Chinese person can state with certainty to which animal his birth year belonged, whether Rat, Ox, Tiger, Hare, Dragon, Snake, Horse, Sheep, Monkey, Fowl, Dog or Pig.

The first historical records which identified the years with the animals in this fashion appeared during the latter part of the Eastern Han dynasty, which ended in 220 A.D. The historian Zhao Yi (1727-1814) concluded that the Han Chinese (who constitute the great majority of all the Chinese people) learned of this concept from the Xiongnu (early forerunners of the Hans) during the Western Han, a period in which there was much contact between the two peoples.

Probably there were originally only four symbols to denote the four directions and four seasons: Dragon — east and spring, Phoenix — south and summer, Tiger — west and autumn, and Tortoise — north and winter. In some unknown fashion these four creatures became the 12 popularly known animals listed above, and in the process each one was assigned either *Yin* (feminine or passive) or *Yang* (masculine or active) qualities.

The foregoing discussion of the origins and historical development of the Chinese calendar will, I hope, serve as a useful background for the readers' understanding of China's traditional festivals. As stated in the foreword, I shall introduce the seven most important festivals in the Chinese tradition.

The Spring Festival or the Chinese Lunar New Year

Origin

It is difficult for the Western mind to grasp the full significance of the Chinese Lunar New Year. On the one hand it was a time for reunion, and at the same time it represented a renewal of the spirit. The Chinese Lunar New Year is followed by the Beginning of Spring. Thus it is a time of renewed fertility of the earth — a wondrous event for ancient man. The New Year, also called the Spring Festival, marked a turning-point in business and one's personal financial affairs as well. All debts had to be paid by this time, and one could hope for a better life and greater success in the coming year.

The New Year was and still is the most widely celebrated festival throughout the whole of China although the name by which it is known has changed several times in the course of history. At one time or another it has been called Time of the Beginning (*Yuan Chen*), First Day (*Yuan Ri*), First Day of the First Month (*Yuan Shuo*), Beginning of the First Month, (*Yuan Zheng*), and First Morning of the Year (*Yuan Dan*).

Now that the Gregorian calendar has been officially adopted, the 1st of January is the official New Year, and the Chinese Lunar New Year has been renamed the Spring Festival (*Chun Jie*).

Festival Preparations in Old China

A thorough house-cleaning used to be undertaken on the 20th day of the bitter month as the 12th month was also called in homes across the breadth of China. Of course, floors were swept regularly in every household, but on this day the heavy closets would be moved away from the walls and the accumulated dust behind swept away. "Be careful when you sweep, my daughter," the old women would caution, "the speck of dust you miss might fly into your eyes and blind you." I was told that in some places one only swept inwards from the outside, lest the family's wealth be swept out of the house.

At this time the well-to-do had their gates repainted, the outer walls whitewashed and the windows freshly papered. Poor people scrubbed and mended the best they could. All this expressed the universal desire to hasten the departure of the outgoing year along with all its misfortunes. Giving the house a complete cleaning on the last day of the year or before has remained a habit in China to this day.

Customs Observed before the New Year

Presents

During the period of time before the New Year known as the "Small New Year", mat sheds would be erected in the main business sections of the city where New Year pictures were sold. Crowds filled the streets as people gathered to enjoy and buy the hothouse-grown flowers displayed in the stalls along with fir branches to ward off evil spirits. Since all shops would soon close for several days, anybody who had the means was out buying presents for friends and relatives, for New Year was the main occasion for exchanging presents. The type of presents given was by and large dictated by convention. Wealthy people gave silks or jewellery to family members; good-quality tea leaves, live flowers, rare fruits or other delicacies to friends or distant relatives. These food presents had both use-value and symbolic value. They implied that the giver did not lack the necessities of life and that he wished to share his abundance. Live poultry and prepared foods were equally appreciated by the recipients.

Almost all businesses and shops closed for business from New Year's Day until as late as the 16th of the month. To buy anything but sweets, peanuts and other small items during the initial post-New Year period was considered unlucky.

The Year-end Settlement of Accounts

In old China the Spring Festival, the Dragon Boat Festival and the Mid-Autumn Festival were the three principal occasions for business establishments, large or small, to balance the books. Between these times many business transactions with relatively poor people but also including some well-off households were conducted on credit, even for such ordinary items like oil, salt, fuel and food.

Debtors unable to pay by the time of Spring Festival often went into hiding from their creditors till New Year's Day. Thus their payment might hopefully be put off until the Dragon Boat Festival. For this very same reason creditors and their agents avidly sought out their debtors on the New

Year's Eve — the last chance to settle. Sometimes they dashed about, lantern in hand, in pursuit of their debtors till the sun rose high in the sky on the morning of New Year's Day. But according to convention, one could no longer demand payment of a debt by that time. At the same time, another convention stipulated that a lantern in one's hand meant that it was still the evening of the previous day and therefore still acceptable to pursue a debtor. Certain parts of town became places of refuge for debtors. The square in front of the Temple of the City God in Beijing was one. As the New Year approached, theatrical troupes performed gratis in honour of the City God. During these performances, even if a debtor chanced to run into his creditors, he was absolutely protected from demands for repayment.

Spring Couplets and New Year Pictures

When the rush of the preparations was over, long strips of red paper were hung up in doorways and elsewhere. These couplets expressed wishes for good luck. At a merchant's doorway one might see "Success in all undertakings" or "Great riches"; at an inn-keeper's, "May customers be as numerous as the clouds"; while peasants hoped for a bountiful harvest. Couplets placed in the home would probably speak of wealth, long life, many sons, or a successful career, and might read, "May all your wishes be fulfilled", or "Ten thousand generations".

Displaying such couplets is an ancient custom dating back to the time when they were written on peachwood boards. During the time of the Five Dynasties and Ten States (907-960), Emperor Meng Chang of the later Shu State had couplets in his own calligraphy hung up on the palace gates.

Later, with the development of paper-making, these peach-wood tablets were replaced by red paper. During the Song dynasty (960-1279) court poets took to writing poems expressing their veneration of the emperor which were then pasted on the walls of the palace. Verses in honour of the New Year did not appear until the Ming dynasty (1368-1644). When the first Ming emperor Hongwu, proclaimed Nanjing the capital, he gave orders to place spring verses on the gate of every house to create a peaceful atmosphere. The emperor wrote the first verse himself and dedicated it to an important official named Tao An. At first only officials wrote these verses, but later on the custom also became widespread among the common people. The themes of the verses were limited to congratulations, praises to spring, and the observance of feudal morality.

I was able to buy some couplets written in the traditional style by a peasant at a country market in Beijing in 1981. One sheet of paper simply bore the single character "Tiger" (I shall refer shortly later to the significance of the tiger). Others carried the words: "The bright moon illuminates the earth", "Clear water ripples over the rocks", "How beautiful are our rivers and mountains", "May you live as long as South Mountain", "May your happiness be as wide as the East Sea". There were other auspicious injunctions such as "Happiness, high position and long life".

In the past people pasted "door gods" on their front gates as a protection against evil spirits. These were colourful woodblock pictures of two guardians in full armour who number among the most ancient of Chinese gods.

Daoist legend has it that two brothers lived under a peachtree so large that five thousand men could hardly encircle it. As protectors of man these two gods vanquished demons which they then threw to the tigers. To commemorate these deeds, district magistrates later set up carved peachwood figures of the two brothers in front of their offices and had tigers painted on the gates. The tiger was considered the sworn enemy of evil spirits, and especially of those who might harm the dead. This is why one often finds tigers on tombs and tombstones in China.

The door gods' identity has long been a subject of disagreement among the various sources. According to the *Shan Hai Jing*, an ancient book on geography which also contains a tremendous amount of information about social practices, legends, and natural science, the door gods are Shen Tu and Yu Lei. Others maintain that these figures actually represents the two Tang generals Qin Shubao and Yuchi Jingde.

When the Tang emperor Tai Zong (r. 627-650) fell ill after his invasion of Korea, evil spirits tormented him every night and the imperial physician could do nothing to help him. Thereupon the two generals came before the emperor in audience. Falling to their knees, they said: "Lord, we have risked our lives many times in the past and killed all your enemies. We are not afraid of evil spirits. Allow us to keep watch tonight and destroy them!" The emperor agreed and the two stood at their post in full armour night after night. The ghosts no longer dared to appear, and the emperor quickly recovered. Tai Zong called the two faithful generals before his presence, saying: "You need no longer sacrifice yourselves, as you, too, need sleep. I hereby order that your portraits be hung up at the palace gates. Thus we shall no longer be troubled by evil spirits." As this evidently worked quite well, the custom was in time adopted by the common folk.

Preparation of Meals

Finally the last day of the 12th month arrived. Enough food had to be prepared beforehand to last for days and to satisfy both man and god, for no knife or other sharp object could be used during the first few days of the New Year lest it cut off the good luck. In addition, the women of the family could then have several days of relative leisure to enjoy the festivities. In south China the favourite and most typical dishes were *nian gao*, sweet steamed glutinous rice pudding, and *zong zi*, another popular delicacy. In the North, steamed wheat bread (*man tou*) and small meat dumplings were the preferred foods. One did not generally eat much meat in a Chinese household, but it was indeed a poor house from which could not be heard the sound of meat being chopped for the filling of the dumplings. If the family had the means, they generally added sweets, copper coins, peanuts, dates and chestnuts to the filling of a few dumplings, and rich families even gold, silver and precious stones. To get one of those dumplings was considered good luck. Copper coins meant that one would never lack money, peanuts stood for long life, dates and chestnuts presaged the imminent arrival of a son because in Chinese the words, "date", and "early", and "chestnut" and "the coming of a son" are homophones. The tremendous amount of food prepared at this time was meant to symbolize abundance and wealth for the household.

The Spring Festival Today

As mentioned earlier, the Lunar New Year, referred to since 1911 as the Spring Festival, is still the most important festival in China. In cities it is observed as an official holiday from the 1st to the 3rd of the first month and in the countryside considerably longer, depending on local work needs. Throughout China it is a time for family reunions, a time for visits with friends, a rest from the hard work of the rest of the year, and all sorts of entertainment. The desire for happiness and prosperity which in the past often found expression in superstitious customs and habits can in many cases still be observed today. The old superstitions, however, have gradually become superfluous. Many old forms have taken on a new meaning. Most people no longer consider the attainment of happiness and fulfilment dependent on spiritual factors. Today's festival is marked by joy in accomplishments and confidence in the future.

A good example of the changes that have taken place can be seen in the New Year pictures, which traditionally were especially popular in the countryside. Folk artists, often peasant families or even whole villages, engaged in the production of these pictures during the winter months when there was not much work to be done in the fields. They would then sell them on the market for a bit of extra money. New Year pictures have probably been made for the last two thousand years. Originally it was customary for the well-to-do to paint the likenesses of legendary heroes or symbols of good luck on the gates of their houses for protection. It was not until woodblock printing was invented and popularized that the New Year picture developed into a people's art. They gained wide popularity around 1500 A.D., during the middle Ming dynasty, and reached their zenith in the 18th century.

These prints were as a rule quite inexpensive. Families usually bought several of them to decorate their homes and to replace those of the previous year. The subjects of the old New Year pictures might be classified into four groups: likenesses of various deities, particularly the Kitchen God and the Guardians of the Gate; scenes from the peasants' lives, very often on a calendar; allegoric or symbolic figures and objects such as peaches, fish, and well-nourished children, all expressing man's desire for a better life, happiness, riches, abundance, many children, long life, fame, and success; scenes from legends, novels, historical episodes and operas.

After 1945 new types of New Year pictures appeared in the revolutionary bases. They preserved the old form, but the contents mirrored the new reality. The old "Guardians of the Gate" were replaced by pairs of peasants, workers or soldiers; instead of the Kitchen God, one found the portrait of Mao Zedong. The New Year pictures of the 1950s depicted traditional as well as modern scenes. On one entitled "Five-fold Riches" there was a fish symbolizing both aquaculture, a common agricultural subsidiary occupation in China, and abundance (abundance is *yu* in Chinese, and fish is also *yu*). The peach not only stands for additional income for the peasant, but is also the symbol for long life. The lotus retains its old meaning of "always, forever".

New Year pictures available nowadays have such motifs as the Guardians of the Gate, the Kitchen God, plump children with fish, peonies, peaches, goldfish, phoenixes with peonies, themes from Chinese operas and scenes from mythology. Others combine the old with the new, such as peasant children and wives carrying baskets full of fish or perhaps lotus blossoms and peaches. In addition, one can also find very modern themes such as the exploration of the universe, but painted in the traditional style.

The content and form of festivals change slowly along with changes in the social systems, not from one day to the next. According to what I was told, the Spring Festival was observed in very much the same way during the "cultural revolution" as before. There were certain differences, however. No pictures of the Kitchen God could be bought, so one painted him oneself and hung up New Year couplets written by oneself. When there were no incense-sticks to be bought, they could be replaced in certain localities with high-quality cigarettes. The persistence of these customs shows that one cannot arbitrarily abolish such festivals. Where a popular basis for the festival exists the people will find a way to realize it.

In 1959 the newspapers carried the official edict that people should no longer honour the Kitchen God, but rather hang up in his stead pictures of workers, peasants, and good harvests. But I was informed in 1980 that incense was still burned and offerings made to the Kitchen God in some villages in the countryside in Shandong Province. Instead of pictures, one saw two scrolls with the couplet "Go up to the sky and then come again bringing good luck." I found no evidence of such practices in Beijing. I think that among the middle-aged and younger generations in the cities, the belief in the old deities has vanished, while the number of country people who still observe the old customs must surely be diminished.

The preparations for the festival still begin around the 23rd day of the 12th month, the day on which the Kitchen God used to be honoured. Already the pace of work is slowing down and all efforts are centred on shopping, making new clothes, and decorating the house. Many young people choose the festival day for their wedding, and children begin setting off firecrackers two weeks before the Spring Festival. A holiday atmosphere gradually develops. As of old, great importance is attached to eating and drinking, and people still favour giving food items as presents. In 1981 there were articles in the newspapers about the shortage of good cigarettes, gin, liquors and jasmine tea for the holidays. On the other hand, on New Year's Day 3.3 million fresh or deep-frozen chickens, one million ducks, as well as vast amounts of lamb, beef and pork were sold in Beijing. As a compensation for the lack of a few items, a sufficient quantity of sweets and toys for the children, radios, televisions and tape-recorders were available, for such items of consumer goods are often purchased at this time of year as a holiday special.

Homes receive a thorough cleaning, the furniture is dusted, and the bedding washed. Offices also come in for a cleaning, and even the city streets are swept with special care. The old superstition that this cleaning would do away with misfortune and bring good luck has since become simply a good habit.

The first day of the Spring Festival fell in 1981 on the 5th of February. On the 2nd of February the street sweepers of Beijing were publicly praised for "their great contribution to public health and hygiene in the capital".

Housewives begin to prepare food dishes two or three days ahead of time. Dumplings are a "must" in north China, of course. When all is prepared, one begins to decorate. Red, yellow-tasselled palace lanterns and streamers with couplets are hung on public buildings. Multi-coloured displays and show windows attract the eye. Today the streamers generally carry only a few words, such as "Spring Festival" or "New Year". In the home people prefer flowers or lanterns. In 1981 Shanghai did an excellent business in narcissi and other flowers as well as silk lanterns, a symbol of good luck, according to a newspaper article on January 31st.

On New Year's Eve everyone tries to be at home. When all the family is together, they usually exchange small presents. For the children there may be some new clothes, toys, sweets or a small sum of money. In old-fashioned families, there are presents for the older people as well, mostly gifts of food for the grandparents and the in-laws. Then comes the feast. In many families a big fish is set on the table, whole, to symbolize the unity of the family. People try to put the best of everything on the table for this occasion, depending on their means. I have noticed that many families then watch television programmes until midnight, this having become a favoured pastime. A variety of programmes are shown, including athletic events and films for children. Or else one might see a play, an opera or some other stage performance. During the 1981 Spring Festival 166 performances of operas, plays, concerts, and ballets were given in Beijing, including 20 performances specifically for children.

The first day of the New Year is devoted to feasting and visiting relatives. On the second or third day friends and acquaintances visit and exchange good wishes.

In recent years shops do business even on holidays. Many people prefer to do their shopping then, for the shops are less crowded. The main occupation of the children is, as always, setting off firecrackers. In contrast to the old times the Spring Festival is now a true festival of joy. Debts, usurious rates of interest, and exorbitant rents need no longer be feared. There was a time when the peasants in Shandong considered it a good year when they could buy enough cloth to patch their old garments. Today every family in the countryside of Anhui Province slaughters a pig for the Spring Festival.

The Lantern Festival

Lantern Festival (*Yuan Xiao Jie*), or the Feast of the First Full Moon, falls on the 15th day of the first lunar month. In olden times the celebrations began several days after the first day of the new year and usually continued until about the 18th, perhaps even longer in certain rural areas, thus bringing the Spring Festival season to a fitting climax. The people of each household celebrated it simply or elaborately in keeping with their financial status and their cultural levels.

Origins and Development

According to certain sources, the Lantern Festival seems to have originated in ancient times as a ceremony to usher in the increasing light and warmth of the sun after the winter's cold; another possibility is that it was originally a ceremony to pray for rains for the spring planting. Historical records from various periods dating back to the Han dynasty (206 B.C.-220 A.D.) reflect the changes in the content of Lantern Festival celebrations over time. During the Han dynasty it was described as an occasion for sacrificial rituals in honour of Tai Yi, the God of the Polar Star, to whom special homage was owed because he embodied the Two Principles of *Yin* and *Yang*, the negative and positive elements, and never changed his position with relation to the rest of the universe. According to Daoist legend, Tai Yi was the elder brother of the founder of Zhou dynasty (C. 1100-256 B.C.)

— a good man whose virtue incurred the cruel vengeance of the last tyrant of the preceding Shang dynasty (C. 1700-1100 B.C.). A much later account from the time of the Southern and Northern dynasties (420-589 A.D.), which describes emperors writing poems in praise of the splendour of the decorated lanterns, shows clearly that the content of Lantern Festival activities had changed from the earlier emphasis on devotional ceremonies. During the last days of the Sui dynasty (581-618 A.D.) Emperor Yang Di, in order to display the richness of the realm, invited many foreign merchants to attend an opera gala in the capital to mark Lantern Festival. Stages were erected on both sides of the city's busiest street for a distance of more than three miles. Three thousand actors and 18 thousand musicians participated in this remarkable series of performances which lasted a full month, with only brief recesses for sleeping and eating.

When Li Shimin, the second emperor and the actual founder of the Tang dynasty, overcame the opposition of all the rival principalities which had sprung up in the wake of the dissolution of the Sui and established the national power of the new Tang dynasty, he suspended all Lantern Festival celebrations for a number of years. With the consolidation of the regime and the emergence of a certain level of prosperity, the ruling class considered that this popular folk festival could serve as an opportunity for the people to display their joy over the restoration of peace and prosperity and for the rulers to share in the pleasures of the common people. Thus it was ordered that celebrations be resumed. In honour of the occasion the government lifted the night time curfew which had been imposed to prevent the common people from revolting. Not only on the night of the festival proper, but also for a few extra days, the populace was

The Lantern Festival

permitted to participate in the celebrations and to view the beautifully-decorated lanterns. During the festival even the emperor, followed by a host of courtiers, joined in the activities.

The description of a certain lantern festival in a book published in 1868 reads: "The sale of fancy paper lanterns preceding the Feast of Lanterns commences usually about the 10th or 11th and reaches its culmination on the evening of the 14th or the 15th. . . . The evening is the time when the largest quantity is exhibited to tempt purchasers and when the streets are more densely crowded with spectators and buyers. . . . Some of the lanterns are cubical, others round like a ball, or circular, square, flat and thin, or oblong, or in the shape of various animals, quadruped and biped. Some are so cunningly constructed as to roll on the ground as a fire-ball; others, such as cocks and horses, are made to go on wheels; still others, when lighted up by a candle or oil, have a rotary or revolving motion of some of their fixtures within. . . . Some are constructed principally of red paper, on which small holes are made in lines, so as to form a Chinese character of auspicious import, as happiness or longevity. These, when lighted up, show the form of the character very plainly. Other lanterns are made in a human shape, and intended to represent children or some objects of worship, as the Goddess of Mercy; some are made to be carried in the hand by means of a handle, others to be placed on a wall or the side of a room. They are gaudily painted with blue, red, and yellow colours, the red usually predominating, as that is a symbol of joy and festivity. The most expensive and the prettiest are covered with white gauze or thin white silk, on which historical scenes or individual characters have been elaborately painted . . . thus adding to one's enjoyment."

The 1936 translation by Derk Bodde of *Annual Customs and Festivals in Beijing*, written by Dun Lichen in 1900, describes the scene at that time. "While all shops display lanterns, it is those of the big streets, as at Dong Si Pailou and Di An Men, which are most numerous. . . . There are variegated lanterns of every colour, made from such material as silk gauze, glass, and transparent horn, which are painted with scenes from old and new legends. . . . Ingenious merchants make objects moulded out of ice, and from young shoots of wheat, pattern figures of men and animals."

In their 1927 book *The Moon Year*, Bredon and Mitrophanow state regretfully: "The old customs are dying out. In Peking, the lantern festival is less brilliant than of old. Gone are the days when a lantern-show in the capital included works of art worth a thousands ounces of silver. . . ."

Festival Customs

In the old days those who were well-off would decorate their houses as brilliantly as possible with lanterns and also set off many firecrackers. There was every variety of fireworks manufactured, such as small boxes, flower pots, fire and smoke rocket poles, "peonies strung on a thread", "lotus sprinkled with water", "falling moons", "grape arbours", "flags of fire", and many others. "Silver flowers" and "fire trees" were perhaps the most popular. Wealthy and prominent households competed with one another in buying fireworks of all types. The usual practice on the evening of the 15th was for a family to offer prayers to certain deities and then to hold a great feast amid revelry and much imbibing. Furthermore, respectable married women were granted greater licence that evening than perhaps any other time. Normally they were confined strictly to their homes; because of Lantern Festival they could go out in the evening to view the display of lanterns.

Many of the customs associated with Lantern Festival have to do with eating, as is true with most of China's traditional festivals. One such custom was known as "eating taro under the lanterns". First a quantity of taro would be boiled till soft. Close to midnight all the members of the family, young and old, male and female, assembled beneath the brightest light suspended high overhead and proceeded to eat the taro provided. Some people said that in this way they could become clear-sighted. Others held that this custom was observed so as to avoid the transmigration of the soul which Buddhists believe follows one's death.

In some cotton-growing regions people used to mould cotton bolls out of wheat flour and stick them in the fields. Then, with burning incense sticks held in their hands, they walked through the fields, hoping by this means to induce a good cotton harvest. Following the completion of the ceremony, the false cotton bolls would be shared among the children in the belief that they would thus be protected from danger.

Yet another food-related custom common both past and present is the eating of *tang yuan*, or *yuan xiao* as it is called in the north, glutinous rice-flour balls with many types of sweet filling in a soup.

In Fujian and other provinces families would light up as many lanterns as the number of family members. To express their desire for more children, they would display many extra lanterns.

Lantern Festival did not of course only mean eating to the

Chinese. There were also many types of colourful and exciting performances for people to enjoy, for example, stilt dance, *yao gu* (waist drum), boat dance, and the donkey dance. Most widespread of all are the dragon dance and lion dance, though the stilt dancers with their carnival spirit were very popular. These were groups of men, some with false beards and painted faces, and others masquerading as women, varying and cavorting about with an amusing gait.

In the Chaozhou and Shantou (Swatow) regions of Guangdong Province swings and merry-go-rounds were common forms of amusements. Said to have originated during the Tang dynasty, these were later introduced to Korea, where young women still follow the custom of playing on swings at the time of Lantern Festival. These practices have long since lost their original religious significance, which had to do with preventing plagues.

The lion dance, perhaps the dance most beloved by the Chinese people, is probably derived from itinerant Indian jugglers and animal trainers who first appeared in China during the Tang dynasty. Since live lions weren't available, a cloth one served their purpose. With one man manipulating the wooden head and another the hindquarters, they developed a dance called the Game of the Lion, which in its earliest form was a demon-expelling ritual. The lion symbolized a Bodhisattva and acted as a guardian of Buddhism.

In China's rural and urban areas, there were many troupes of lion dancers parading through the streets or going from village to village. Each troupe might be composed of one or two lions, two other dancers luring them on with large embroidered balls in lieu of pearls, and some musicians beating on gongs and drums.

In modern China the most likely place a city dweller

would be able to see the lion dance would be at an acrobatic performance. To the delight of the spectators, the blue and yellow lions dance, roll, and jump about on stage in pursuit of the "pearls", displaying remarkable agility with eyeballs rolling, tongues flopping, jaws clacking and bells tinkling.

A literary game that was once very popular among the older educated classes on the evening of the 15th day was called Guessing the Lantern's Riddle (*Cai Deng Mi*). A number of riddles would first be written on slips of paper which were then pasted lightly onto lanterns suspended either in front of the house or inside. If required by particular riddles, certain clues could sometimes be hung from the lanterns. These were called *Mi Mian* (the riddle's face) and had written upon them a clue to the correct solution of the riddle, such as a Chinese character, a line of verse, the name of a well-known person, or a place name. Anyone who guessed correctly was rewarded on the spot. Often the riddles were very obscure allusions which were extremely difficult to decipher. Foreigners, even those well-versed in Chinese literature and affairs, would almost certainly be at a loss to answer correctly.

Changes Since 1949

Nowadays there is no official Lantern Festival vacation. During the 1950s amateur performances of many of the traditional dance and other activities continued to be carried out in the countryside, generally organized by the production brigades on the people's communes.

With the advent of the "cultural revolution" in the latter part of the 1960s, many ways of expressing traditional

Chinese culture, including the performances mentioned above, were attacked because of their supposed feudal, capitalist, or revisionist content. Even the actors' costumes and paraphernalia were destroyed. After the downfall of the Gang of Four performances and other activities in celebration of Lantern Festival were resumed.

In 1981 Lantern Festival came on February 19. The snowfall that morning was taken as an auspicious omen of a coming bumper harvest.

Many different programmes were scheduled. At the Children's Palace in Beijing some children stood with lanterns in their hands, others danced around them, while still others set off firecrackers. One could also enjoy Peking Opera, *qu yi* (a category of folk art forms including ballad singing, story telling, comic dialogues, clapper talks, and cross talks), puppet shows, calligraphy and painting exhibitions, including New Year pictures, and ship and plane model displays. All of these activities were organized by young people.

The Pure Brightness Festival

Conducting ancestor worship ceremonies on the day of the Pure Brightness Festival is a time-honoured tradition among the Chinese people. At the time of its earliest appearance the festival was on the third day of the third month of the Chinese lunar calendar; for reasons unknown to us now, its timing at some point came to be based rather on the system of solar terms. Pure Brightness is the fifth of the 24 solar terms. When translated into the Gregorian calendar, it begins on either the 4th or 5th of April. Another way of looking at it is to say that both the festival Pure Brightness and the first day of the solar term of the same name come on the 106th day after the winter solstice.

As the name suggests, the day is thought generally to be a clear and bright one. The *Qing Ming* Festival, as it is called in Chinese, was originally a celebration of nature's emergence from its long winter dormancy. People would take the opportunity to go on excursions outside the city. "Treading the green grass" was how they described it.

The Chinese conception of ancestor worship is born of a belief that the spirit survives the body after death and is aware of the conduct of those left behind. To the Chinese mind, the spirit's powers, for good or for ill, are superior to both man and nature. Perhaps in their anxiety to pacify these supernatural beings lies the origin of the annual ceremonies based around the gravesite at the time of the "rebirth" of nature.

Immediately after breakfast on *Qing Ming* entire families, hoes and other tools in hand, would start arriving at the foothills outside their villages, where they would commence to diligently tidy up the area around their family's tomb. Yellow ribbons were placed on the end of a bamboo stick or kept in place by a stone on top of the tomb so as to stave off wandering ghosts. These malevolent spirits perhaps had been neglected by their descendants or, alternatively, may have died in such a fashion as to make recovery of the body impossible, thus being doomed to eternal wandering. Innumerable Chinese tales revolve around these homeless ghosts' capacity for mischief.

A passage from an old book describes how a well-to-do family in pre-1949 Fuzhou, the capital of Fujian Province, conducted the *Qing Ming* grave-sweeping ceremonies. "The festival arrives with all necessary preparations completed. The family arrives at the tomb site, which is dominated by a large semi-circular altar standing in the foreground. They place offerings of food, tea, and wine together with candles on each side of the altar or before the gravestone; an incense burner claims pride of place at the altar.

"The burning of incense and candles signals the beginning of the ceremony. Each male member of the household performs in turn the kowtow — the ritual of three prostrations and three bows, accompanied by the explosions of firecrackers. A libation of wine is sprinkled over burning paper money, and then the cup is refilled and put back in place. Next follows a repetition of the kowtow. The offerings of food may either be consumed then and there or taken home. The ceremony comes to an end as more firecrackers are set off. Back at home they make offerings again before the family's ancestral tablet of food, candles, incense, and a few evergreen sprigs or heads of wheat, all arranged neatly on a platter."

The Pure Brightness Festival

A passage from Lu Xun's story, *Medicine*, suggests a contrasting picture of the festival as experienced by an ordinary family in the late Qing dynasty.

"*Qing Ming* this year is unusually cold, though the willows have already put out shoots as big as half a grain of rice. Shortly before sunrise the woman placed four dishes of food and a bowl of rice before her child's fresh grave and cried out her prayers. After burning some paper money, she slumped back on her heels and sank into a stupor."

It was generally believed that, by burning paper money, the living could assure the departed of an income in the next world; in the old China the children of a deceased man of wealth would even send him gold and silver ingots, servants, horses and sedan-chairs, all in paper imitation, to secure his welfare.

In the time of imperial China emperors, high officials, and the very rich prepared their eternal resting-places during their prime of life. Their magnificent mausoleums were usually flanked by temples, pavilions, towers, and beautiful gardens, with servants or, in the case of an emperor, imperial concubines, appointed as caretakers. Imperial coffin chambers of course were especially well-endowed with all that the departed one could require to ensure an underground version of his previous life in the palace. Pottery figurines, gold and silver sacrificial utensils, a wealth of foodstuffs, embroidered silks, and elaborate hardware — all were included, and more.

The traditional method of choosing a tombsite among the Chinese was according to the principles of geomancy, the science of "wind and water". The instructions of the geomancer had to be strictly observed in order to ensure good fortune and prosperity to come. The common folk had to content themselves with a burial plot in their own family properties or in the hilly wilderness, while the rich could afford a wide search for a suitable location. In case the hunt dragged on, a Buddhist or ancestral temple could be utilized for temporary storage of the coffin.

Another name for *Qing Ming* Festival is "Cold Food Day". This appellation applied originally to the preceding day, when people could eat only cold food. Cooking on that day was considered to be taboo. Although this practice has long been neglected, the legend surrounding its origin, which dates back to the State of Jin (present day Shanxi Province together with parts of Henan and Shaanxi) during the Spring and Autumn Period (770-475 B.C.), is a well-known one among the Chinese and thus might be interesting to relate in some detail.

Toward the end of his reign the Jin ruler Duke Xian was taken in by his second wife Li Ji's vicious slander, so he declared her son Xi Qi his successor, rather than the eldest of his three sons by his previous wife, all of whom he now ordered killed. The eldest brother, Shensheng, cut his own throat thus sacrificing himself to the ideal of filial piety. His two brothers, Zhonger and Yiwu, fled into exile. After enduring 19 years of hardships Zhonger regained the throne with the military assistance of the neighbouring State of Qin. But just when Zhonger and his retinue were returning to the capital, the company began to break up. It was started by Huyan, Zhonger's uncle when they reached the banks of the Yellow River. Hoping to gain higher position in the new regime, he declared with false modesty, "In all my years of services I've committed too many offences, I'm afraid. I believe you'll never be able to forgive me." Then he pleaded, "Now that you're assured of the crown, I beg to take my leave. That way I could feel less ashamed of myself."

"May the God of the River take me if I should share with you only the woe but not the weal," swore Zhonger in his effort to dissuade him. As a token of his determination, he threw a jade pendant into the water.

One of Huyan's colleagues, Jie Zitui, was immensely annoyed by the whole scene.

"It's by the grace of Heaven that His Highness has got his crown, yet you attempt to take all the credit and even try to wrest some kind of promise from him by threatening to quit," he said in scornful disapproval. "How ashamed I feel for you."

Jie Zitui was further aggravated by another member of the company who without further ado threw all of their cooking utensils and other gear into the river, as if hoping with one stroke to blot out the bitter lessons of the past years. This was too much for Jie Zitui to bear so that no sooner had Zhonger returned to the capital than Jie Zitui walked out, leaving it all behind. Though Zhonger did later remember to reward his companions in exile, he completely forgot Jie Zitui despite his years of loyal service. There had even been a time when Jie Zitui saved his lord from starvation by giving him a piece of meat cut from Jie Zitui's own leg!

When several of the ministers to Zhonger's court presented a memorial protesting the shoddy treatment shown Jie Zitui, Zhonger saw the error of his ways and sent people to search for him. Jie Zitui fled, however, bearing his mother on his back. He hid deep within the forests of Mount Mian. In an attempt to smoke them out, Zhonger ordered a fire started. When the fire had burned itself out after three days and three nights, mother and son were found as they had died, with their arms thrown around a willow tree. A grieving Zhonger ordered that Mount Mian be renamed Mount Jie and also that Jie Zitui's hometown should be called Jie Xiu (Jie's Resting Place). He also commanded that a shrine be built for mother and son to keep alive their memory. In the ensuing ages it gradually grew into a popular custom that on the day of Jie Zitui's death no fire must be lit, but willow branches were to be gathered and planted in front of each family's home. This, then, is the origin of Cold Food Day.

Kite-Flying and other Qing Ming Activities

In ancient times *Qing Ming* Festival was the time for many more activities than simply performing the grave-sweeping ceremonies. These included various kinds of ball games, cockfighting, dog racing, swings, and other entertainment.

During the Song dynasty (960-1279) there emerged a new custom which involved hanging the figure of a flying swallow made of flour and dates from a willow branch in the doorway of one's home. These were called "Zitui Swallows": both the name and the willow branch harked back to the unfortunate Jie Zitui. Children would also offer flour swallows, boiled eggs and gold and silver ingots in paper imitation to the village god.

Judging by its great popularity through much of Chinese history, kite-flying appears to have particularly caught the Chinese fancy. This sport can be traced all the way back to the Warring States period (475-221 B.C.) and has been a popular theme in Chinese tales ever since. Mo Di, a philosopher of the early Warring States period, made many attempts at constructing a wooden kite and is said to have finally succeeded at the end of the third year. Another version of the story credits the honour of having invented the first kite to Mo Di's contemporary Lu Ban, the legendary master carpenter. Whichever was the case, however, the technique was lost in subsequent centuries.

A later version attributes the creation of the kite to Han Xin, a famous general of the Western Han dynasty. It came to be known as the Paper Hawk because it was fashioned of a bamboo skeleton wrapped in paper or silk in the shape of a bird. This style of kite was frequently employed for military purposes. During the reign of Emperor Wu Di (502-550 A.D.) in the Southern and Northern dynasties period (420-589), the city of Tai was once surrounded and attacked by a rebellious army. The Crown Prince Xiao Gang used a kite to signal for help. Later on during the Five Dynasties and the Ten States period (907-960), the kite was further improved upon by Li Ye, who adapted a whistle for the kite which produced a sound like that of the *zheng*, an ancient zither-like stringed musical instrument. There lies the origin of the modern name for the kite; *feng zheng* — wind zither.

As the techniques of kite-making were gradually perfected, the kite came into its own with an enormous variety of shapes: butterflies, frogs, centipedes, carp, stars, the moon, and many different historical or legendary figures such as the Monkey King. Kite-flying has long since ceased to be peculiar to *Qing Ming* alone and was and can now be seen the year round anytime there happens a fine breezy day.

The Modern Qing Ming Festival

The radical changes in China's social system since 1949 have obviously had a major impact upon Chinese cultural life. *Qing Ming* has been no exception to this rule. Cremation as a means of disposing of the dead is now virtually universal in China's cities. Many crematories have been constructed where the dead are burned and their ashes stored, usually for a period of not more than five years. Out of religious consideration members of the Hui minority nationality, who practise the Islamic religion, are exempted from the law requiring cremation in the cities.

In China's cities traditional ancestor worship ceremonies are largely a thing of the past and are now confined mainly to a few state-run public graveyards and monuments. The modern *Qing Ming* Festival has been recast as a day of patriotism. During my stay in Beijing, for instance, I witnessed the presentation of memorial wreaths to heroes of the Chinese revolution by relatives and primary school children at the Babaoshan Cemetery and the Tian'anmen Square Monument of the People's Heroes.

In the vast countryside, however, tradition dies hard. Burial continues to be widely practised. *Qing Ming* is still the time for families to visit their family gravesite, and in many places people burn paper money and make simple offerings. The major difference is that public graveyards are now the norm, and no land that can be used for productive purposes may be occupied by graves. The 1981 festival witnessed the revival of an extremely ancient memorial ceremony in honour of the Yellow Emperor, who is considered to be the foremost ancestor of the Chinese

The Pure Brightness Festival

people. This ceremony occurred in Huangling County, Shaanxi Province, at the site which is reputed to be the gravesite of this legendary figure in Chinese history.

The Dragon Boat Festival

Origin and Legends

The Dragon Boat Festival, or *Duan Wu Jie*, falls on the fifth day of the fifth lunar month. It is also known as *Duan Yang*, the Upright Sun, or Double Fifth. Among the Chinese, however, it used to be most commonly known as the Fifth Month Festival. The festival is in the midst of the summer season; the weather is quite hot, with frequent rain showers, yet there are also many days of fine weather at this time of year. Quiet prevails in the villages except for the shrilling cicadas, as the farmers are on the verge of the season's first harvest.

The Dragon Boat Festival comes just around the time of the Summer Solstice. We have a custom in Germany today, as in the past, of gathering firewood together on the grasslands the night of the Summer Solstice, then setting it on fire at dusk the following day. Sometimes a demon constructed of straw and rag is placed on the fire. Some old people claim that one's every prayer that night will come true. In contrast, a book on ritual written in the latter part of the Eastern Han dynasty referred to the prohibition of any "visible fire" on the Summer Solstice.

In earliest times the Summer Solstice was in many disparate human societies intimately connected with sacrificial ceremonies relating to certain crucial social activities, such as hunting, fishing and tribal warfare. In ancient China most people lived in the river valleys, so these ceremonies evolved into practices specifically aimed to propitiate the River God. People considered the rivers to be controlled by a dragon who also determined the distribution of rain water for agriculture and human subsistence. Sacrifices were therefore offered to the dragon on the Summer Solstice, which precedes the arrival of the rainy season in the sixth lunar month, in the hope of being favoured by timely rainfall with neither drought nor flood. Thus the Chinese people adopted the dragon as both deity and totem, not only among the Han majority nationality, but also among some of the minority peoples in the South.

Duan Wu Jie, the Dragon Boat Festival, developed from its actual origins as a means to propitiate the river dragon, to what it later became in the popular mind, namely, a festival to commemorate Qu Yuan, the great poet and patriotic political figure of the State of Chu during the Warring States period. Born in 340 B.C., Qu Yuan was a member of one of the three important noble families which shared power at the Chu imperial court. Qu Yuan was the king's trusted counsellor, issuing decrees and receiving state guests on behalf of King Huai who reigned from 328 to 299 B.C.

During the Warring States period China was marked by the appearance of a number of contending kingdoms existing in a state of confrontation, war, and instable alliances. The states, which were all striving for domination, were Qi, Chu, Yan, Wei, Zhao, Han and Qin. Qin, whose territory was mainly in the present-day Shaanxi Province and environs, was the strongest power (and in fact the last ruler of the State of Qin succeeded in 221 B.C. in establishing the Qin dynasty, the first unified empire in Chinese history). Chu, located along the Yangtze River, had the largest area among the seven states and was consequently Qin's foremost enemy. Chu's territory extended from the shores of the East China Sea westwards all the way to southern Sichuan, and including today's Hunan, Hubei, Anhui, Zhejiang and Jiangxi provinces. The State of Qi, located on the coast of the East China Sea, was the richest owing to its development of fishery and salt production. Since Qi was located far from Qin, the latter was in no hurry to annex it. Han, Zhao and Wei, situated in the middle reaches of the Yellow River, were comparatively weak, and Yan in northwest China was almost entirely out of the arena of warfare.

Consequently, the three states of Qin, Chu and Qi constituted the most powerful belligerent forces. Chu and Qi formed an alliance to resist Qin, which the latter tried its best to sabotage in order to attain hegemony over the entire country. Qin's plan was to defeat and absorb first the State of Chu, and then all the other states one by one.

Qu Yuan realized that Qin was the greatest menace to Chu. He therefore submitted a memorial to King Huai proposing the establishment of an anti-Qin alliance with Han, Wei and Qi. However, a number of other important ministers to the imperial court, including Premier Zi Jiao, Jin Shang, and the King's favourite concubine Zheng Xiu, opposed Qu Yuan's proposal. Their view was that, because Qin was the most powerful state, Chu should rather form an alliance with it and above all not offend it in anyway. Thus could the other states be induced to come over to Qin and Chu, they hoped, and confrontation avoided as well.

These influential figures in the imperial court sowed discord between King Huai and Qu Yuan, causing the King to lose trust in the loyal Qu Yuan. A short-lived alliance between Qin and Chu dissolved immediately when Qin declared war on Chu. The latter suffered many defeats and lost huge tracts of territory. In the midst of the fighting, Qin proposed that the Chu monarch come to Qin for cease-fire negotiations. Despite Qu Yuan's warnings King Huai insisted on going and, in the 30th year of his reign, was taken captive. Qin promised to set the King free only at the expense of the cession of territory. Three years later the unfortunate monarch died in prison. The eldest son, King Qing Xiang (whose reign ultimately ran from 299-263 B.C.), ascended the throne and appointed his younger brother Zi Lan premier. The new premier knew only the pursuit of pleasure; thus, the imperial administration became ever more corrupt and the situation of the state ever more desperate.

As Qu Yuan witnessed the destruction of his motherland at the hands of these corrupt and incompetent ministers, he could no longer remain silent, expressing his rage and melancholy through poetry. Premier Zi Lan seized the chance to slander Qu Yuan before the throne and as a result, Qu Yuan was banished from Ying, the capital of Chu, in the year 286 B.C. Crossing over the Yangtze River, he led a wandering life in the vicinity of Dongting Lake and the Milo River, not far from Changsha, Hunan. During his sojourn there he wrote many outstanding poems rich in romanticism and evocative of the atmosphere of south China. Qu Yuan's poetry clearly expresses his patriotic feelings and the power of his imagination. Amongst his most famous works are *Li Sao* in which he revealed his political aspirations, *Jiu Ge* (*Nine Songs*) which he adapted from the folksong style, *Tian Wen* and many others. The beauty and grace of his poetry have secured for him a prominent place among China's most beloved poets.

In the second month of the year 278 B.C., the armies of Qin, led by General Bai Qi, occupied Ying, razing the imperial palace and ruling family's ancestral temple to the ground. Upon hearing the ill tidings three months later, Qu Yuan, in great sorrow and distress, jumped into the Milo River holding a large stone, thus giving his life for his country. This sad event took place on the fifth day of the fifth month.

Because of Qu Yuan's ardent love for his country and people, he had gained the love and respect of the people. When they learned of his death, many people rowed out to the spot to search for his body, but without success. Such is the origin of dragon boat racing which, at least according to popular legend, has been held every year since then on the fifth day of the fifth month to honour the memory of Qu Yuan. The races and the festival as well are in truth the product of the integration of stories concerning Qu Yuan with ancient Summer Solstice rituals aimed at propitiating the river dragon. The actual dragon boat races quite possibly pre-dated Qu Yuan's time, according to some reports starting as early as the Spring and Autumn period (770-476 B.C.) in the State of Yue when King Gou Jian used boat races to train his naval forces.

In the historical records from the first part of the Han dynasty (206 B.C.-220 A.D.) can be found no mention of Qu Yuan's death nor any connection between the holding of dragon boat races and the fifth day of the fifth month. It was not until the second century A.D. that people linked Qu Yuan's death with that particular day. And dragon boat racing as a widely-practised festival activity did not become prevalent until the Tang dynasty (618-907), by which time it had spread throughout the Yangtze River valley to most of south China. Since then it has remained a custom largely of the south; in those areas the races mark the climax of several days of gay festivities.

The boats used for the dragon boat races have a very narrow width and can be up to 30 metres long. The boat's prow is formed by a magnificently carved wooden dragon head. Each boat will have eight to fifteen pairs of oarsmen. In some regions the oarsmen sit down, using short oars while in others the oarsmen stand and use long oars. In the boat's middle section stand two men, one beating a drum and the other a gong. Another man at the prow synchronizes the strokes of the oarsmen by waving a small red flag and chanting out work songs. The spectators massed on the banks shout out their encouragement.

Of all the customs associated with the Dragon Boat Festival, possibly the most wide spread is the preparation and eating of *zong zi*, leaf-wrapped glutinous rice balls with various kinds of filling. The story behind *zong zi* also goes back to Qu Yuan's death. After the poet had killed himself, people cast sections of bamboo filled with rice into the river to honour his soul. His spirit, however, was not satisfied with this practice, according to a popular legend. During the reign of Jianwu (26-55 A.D.) of the Eastern Han dynasty a man from Changsha named Ou Hui was confronted by the spirit of Qu Yuan who told him that the rice-filled bamboo offerings were being devoured by the river dragon before he could get them. The proper method, said the spirit, was to wrap the bamboo sections in chinaberry leaves and to close the opening with silk threads in five colours, as the dragon would thus not dare to interfere (for unexplained reasons).

Ou Hui did as he was told and this in time became the accepted custom.

The earliest *zong zi*, I presume, did indeed take the form of a rice-filled bamboo section, but the term was not then used. The people of that region cooked rice in bamboo as a regular practice. Even today the Zhuang and Dai minorities in south China and the Vietnamese and Thai people continue to make use of bamboo sections in this way. The rice thus prepared is said to be particularly tasty. Later on palm leaves were used to wrap rice, green beans, peanuts and dates into pyramid-shaped dumplings. Only from that time on did the name *zong zi* appear, because *zong* is a homonym of the written character for palm.

What then is the connection between the dragon boat and the dragon of ancient Chinese religious beliefs? It is said that the fishermen from the states of Wu (now Jiangsu Province) and Yue (now Zhejiang Province) during the Spring and Autumn period shaved their heads and covered their bodies with tattoos in the hope that by posing as dragons, they could be saved from mishap by the dragons, which presumably would mistake them for their own kind. Each year sacrificial rites were held in honour of the dragon god. Using dragon shaped boats was both a way to please the dragon god and also, when races were first introduced as a kind of amusement in the Han dynasty, a popular sport.

Dragons of the East and West

The dragon is not the subject of legends only among the Chinese. One finds it referred to in the tales of many nations. In the West it was regarded as an amalgamation of bird, snake and lion and in many fairy tales is often depicted as a fire-breathing creature with many heads.

According to the findings of Wen Yiduo (1899-1946), a noted Chinese scholar and poet, the Chinese conception of the dragon is rooted in its early function as a totem, an imaginary symbol of a clan or tribe. Among the primitive tribes in China, some worshipped the snake, others the bird and still others the dog, fish, deer, or other animals. After the amalgamation of some of these tribes their totems underwent a metamorphosis as well; the snake tribe was dominent, however, in both the temporal and the totemic planes. Thus the image of the dragon was based on the body of the snake, the head, mane and tail of the horse, the horns of the deer, the paws of the dog, the scales and whiskers of the fish and the wings of the bird.

In the West the dragon represented an evil force, sometimes an anti-Christ, which could cause floods, swallow the sun and the moon and threaten the Virgin Mary; only by killing it could the world's existence be ensured. Dragons even appeared in the Old Testament in the form of the re-appearance of a prehistorical snake-like monster which threatened the existence of mankind. North German fairy tales and poems from the Middle Ages and other European folktales contained dragons which generally were depicted as a monstrous boa or lizard. In legends concerning the German heroes, the killing of a dragon is proof of a heroic spirit. In this connection, the reader may recall stories about the dragon-slaying exploits of Sigmund, his son Siegfried, Beowulf, and Dietrich von Bern. St. George was another prominent scourge of dragons, according to legend. Struggles with dragons are often the themes of children's stories. In many German folktales some dragon-like creatures appear as the guardians of treasures stored within caves. Quite a number of place names in Germany retain hints of such legends, for example, Drachenfels (Dragon Rock), Drachenwand (Dragon Wall) and Drachenloch (Dragon Cave). Overall it could be said that in the West the dragon is usually symbolic of devilry, ferocity, and sin.

In China the dragon came to be conceptualized in an entirely different way than in the West. It was essentially regarded as a benevolent deity that bestowed good fortune upon mankind. It ruled the rivers and seas and dominated the clouds and rains as well. Thus the dragon quite naturally became an object of worship by people in traditional China, and it was the dragon to whom people prayed when making offerings for a bumper harvest. The dragon manifests itself, according to the old belief, once every 12th hour, every 12th month and every 12th year.

Despite the great differences between the Western and Chinese dragons as described above, there are two points of similarity. One is the similarity in appearance, and the other is that both are connected with water. The ancient Greeks believed, however, that the dragon was responsible for the periodic floods.

Additional Festival Customs

Many of the other customs that have always been associated with the Dragon Boat Festival have to do with the fact that the fifth month is held to be the "Evil Month", the time of hot, steamy weather which facilitates the growth of harmful insects and germs and contributes to the spread of infectious diseases. For the purpose of expelling the gods of plague, people pasted both inside and outside the house strips of yellow paper of varied lengths inscribed with

The Dragon Boat Festival

incantations and printed with the images of certain animal-shaped deities. Many people also burned realgar, a reddish mineral which burns with a yellow smoke and a foul odour. It was considered to have the power to exterminate insects. In many places old women would cut red paper into the shapes of the "five poisonous creatures" (scorpion, viper, centipede, house lizard and spider) and place them, together with a cut-paper tiger, into a gourd, thus implying that all poisonous creatures and fierce beasts were confined within and so unable to harm human beings. During festival time girls wore a "fragrant pouch" made of bits of cloth wound round with coloured silk threads. In some areas these became a highly developed form of local handicrafts.

Come Dragon Boat Festival time, some shops in Beijing used to sell foot-long strips of yellow paper embossed with a scarlet seal (the colour scarlet was believed helpful in dispelling ghosts), pictures showing Zhong Kui gobbling up the "five ghosts"), or the image of Zhong Kui alone. On sale also were cakes in the shape of the five poisonous creatures; people believed that symbolic poison could be employed as an antidote for the real thing and that the image of evil could be used to combat evil. Therefore eating cakes shaped like poisonous creatures would protect one from harm.

Who now was Zhong Kui, and why was he presented as an image to quell the five poisonous creatures? Of course there is a story behind it, as we shall now hear. Emperor Ming Huang (reigned 712-756) of the Tang dynasty one day came down with a high temperature. In his dream he was confronted by a demon. Suddenly a tall but extremely ugly figure holding a wooden sword appeared before the emperor and proceeded to gouge out and swallow one of the demon's eyes. In response to the emperor's enquiry, this man revealed himself to be Zhong Kui, a scholar from the previous dynasty who, upon failing the imperial examination because of his ugly appearance, committed suicide. He had sworn to slay all demons in the other world so as to protect the emperor and decent people. Awaking from his dream, the emperor found that his high temperature had disappeared. He therefore ordered a court artisan to paint an image based on his descriptions of Zhong Kui and bestowed upon him the title of "Great Demon-Expelling General".

The usual custom was to place food platters together with realgar wine side by side on the altar and to burn incense before the images of the deities and the family's own ancestral tablets. The realgar wine, mixed with cinnabar, would then be spread over the ears, nose and forehead of a male child to exorcise any lurking evil spirits.

Realgar compounds have in fact definite disinfectant qualities. Realgar wine is also said to be good for one's health, and this too has a certain scientific basis. Another example of a popular custom with a sound medical basis is that of hanging Chinese mugwort leaves, calamus, or garlic in the doorway in order to prevent plagues.

At this juncture I can cite two similar customs in Europe. On the night of June 24, the birthday of Johannes des Taufers (just after the Summer Solstice), Russian peasants used to place straw and wood on the rooftops of their homes and cattle sheds. They believed that the straw, which was called "Johannes Pflanzen", could disperse demons. In the north of France people hung "sacred Johannes Pflanzen", a mixture of mugwort and other grasses on their door steps and cattle sheds.

Before 1949 the Dragon Boat Festival was observed in some parts of the country as an official holiday by schools, government institutions and banks. Shops suspended business in the afternoon. People could thus watch the dragon boat races or take part in other holiday activities. In Guangdong, known as the "land of music", musical performances were held aboard boats. Among the well-to-do, the festival was an occasion for feasts and the exchanging of gifts. As far as the poor were concerned, the festival was not necessarily a joyful occasion, for it was one of three times throughout the year when debts had to be settled. In the north the festival comes at the same time as the wheat harvest, and in the south it is close to the rice harvest. If the harvest were poor, could the poor people celebrate the festival with joy?

The Dragon Boat Festival Today

On the day of the festival in modern-day China people go to work as usual. Yet, the deeds of Qu Yuan are ever more disseminated and eulogized. People hold this great patriot in great respect. Newspapers carry many articles in commemoration of Qu Yuan; on one occasion that I saw, a special supplement was published by one of the newspapers. Qu Yuan's poetry is very popular, and the scholarly critical literature is quite considerable.

Though festival activities are much less than in the past, dragon boat races are still conducted on an extensive scale in the south; eating *zong zi* becomes evermore popular throughout the country. Food shops supply this festival favourite, but many families prefer to make their own *zong zi*. Superstitious activities are no longer much in evidence. Realgar wine is seldom drunk these days, but in some families, the display of mugwort and calamus leaves is continued. In 1981, I was able to buy a variety of cloth figures embroidered with threads in five colours and cloth tigers filled with fragrant herbs, but these are taken only as articles of decorative art.

The Mid-Autumn Festival

An Overview

The Mid-Autumn or Moon Festival is one rich in poetic significance. Ancient legends that became interwoven with this festival's celebration further contribute to the warm regard in which it has always been held by the Chinese people. According to the lunar calendar, the seventh, eighth, and ninth months constitute the autumn season. Mid-Autumn Festival falls on the 15th day of the eighth lunar month, precisely in the middle of this season, when the heat of the summer has given way to cool autumn weather, marked by blue skies and gentle breezes. On this day the moon is at its greatest distance from the earth; at no other time is it so luminous. Then, as the Chinese say, "The moon is perfectly round." In the villages the heavy work involved in the summer harvest has already been completed but the autumn harvest has not yet arrived.

The actual origins of the Mid-Autumn Festival are unclear. The earliest records are from the time of the great Han dynasty emperor Wu Di (156-87 B.C.), who initiated celebrations lasting three days, including banquets and "Viewing the Moon" evenings on the Toad Terrace (the story behind this toad follows shortly). We know that people during the Jin dynasty (265-420 A.D.) continued the custom of Mid-Autumn Festival celebrations, and similar accounts have come down to us from the time of the Tang dynasty. During the Ming dynasty (1368-1644) houses and gardens were decorated with numerous lanterns, and the sound of gongs and drums filled the air.

Myths and Legends

The moon has from the dawn of time been an object of supreme fascination for mankind. In human societies all over the world innumerable legends surround the moon and its origins. We can easily imagine early shepherds watching their flocks, or the nomads who lived their lives out in the open, lying on the ground at night, gazing up at the moon. Their imaginations played upon the shadows visible on the moon's surface, and as they talked among themselves, the myths which have been handed down to the present day gradually took shape.

The regularity of the waxing and waning of the moon has always intrigued people to the extent that many phenomena in nature and in human existence, such as the fertility of man and animal, illness and health, birth and death and love and marriage, are even now frequently ascribed to the influence of the moon. Among peasants, particularly, the phases of the moon were taken into consideration for the determination of the correct time for sowing and harvesting the crops or for animal-breeding. The time of the waning moon was feared as being especially inauspicious. Many other superstitious beliefs were associated with the time of the new moon or the full moon. The moon was worshipped as a deity by many ancient peoples: in Babylon as Sin, in Egypt as Thot, in Greece as Selene and among the Romans as Luna.

It is intriguing to note that the theme of a rabbit inhabiting the moon is a common thread running through the mythology of many peoples around the world, including the Chinese. In India people believed that a rabbit being chased by a dog escaped to the moon.

The Hottentots and certain other southern African tribes tell the story that long ago the moon chose the rabbit as its emissary to tell mankind that they must die but would then rise from the dead. The rabbit started on his journey in great haste, arriving so out of breath that he garbled the message, saying: "When you die, you will remain dead forever." This news plunged men deep into sorrow until the tortoise who, as the second emissary, had naturally plodded along much more slowly, delivered accurately the message of immortality. Those who had believed the rabbit were so angry that they wanted to kill it; one hurled a stone which struck the rabbit just below its mouth. This is why the rabbit to this day has a harelip. Thereupon, the rabbit, in fury and pain, fled to the moon.

The connection between the moon and rabbit is clearly a very ancient one. In classical Greece the rabbit was considered to be the reincarnation of Artemis, the Goddess of Hunting, and also of Aphrodite, the Goddess of Love. The rabbit, as an easy prey for other animals, was regarded as a hunted creature which could only ensure its survival through proliferation; thus it became symbol of fertility, existence and happiness.

The concept of a moon rabbit was introduced to China with the advent of the Indian Buddhist influence, as related in the following story: Once upon a time there was a forest glade to which holy men often came to meditate. It contained a wonderful garden with fruits and flowers, tender grasses, and the rippling waters of a shining stream. In this small paradise there lived a rabbit whose virtues outshone those of all other living things.

One evening the Buddha, accompanied by several of his diciples, came to the garden. They sat at his feet and listened to his recitation of the sutras. So passed a night and a day until the scorching sun stood in the sky and the cicadas shrilled. It was the time when every creature sought the shade and every traveller suffered from the heat.

Buddha assumed the form of a Brahman and called out sorrowfully: "I am alone, my friends have abandoned me and I am hungry and thirsty. Believers, come and help me!" The small animals of the forest heard his call and one after another hastened to his side.

They begged him to stay and accept their hospitality. Each brought such food as it could. The otter brought seven fish and said: "Take these and stay with us." The jackal brought part of his prey and asked Buddha to honour them with his presence and be their teacher. Then came the turn of the rabbit. He modestly stepped forward, his hands empty. "Master! I have grown up in the woods. Herbs and grasses are my food. I have nothing else to offer you but my body. Bless us and rest here, and feed on my gladly proffered flesh, for there is nothing else I can give you." Just then the rabbit caught sight of some magic coal, coal that burns without smoke. Just as he was about to jump into the flames, he stopped suddenly and picked the tiny insects out of its fur, saying: "I may give my body to the saint, but I have no right to take your lives." Setting the insects carefully on the ground, the rabbit threw himself into the fire.

Buddha resumed his own form and praised the sacrifice: "He who forgets himself, the most modest of all earthly creatures, shall reach the Ocean of Eternal Peace! All men should learn from him and be as compassionate and helpful as he!" Buddha then gave instructions that the likeness of the rabbit should adorn the moon and thus remain a shining example for all time. And thanks to their holy friend, all the animals in the forest were placed in the world of saints.

Daoism, the indigenous religion of China, adopted the rabbit in the moon along with many other concepts that originated in Buddhism. They called it the Jade Rabbit and pictured it with short front paws, very long back legs and a short tail. It is said to stand under a magical cassia tree on the moon making pills of immortality, also known as the jade elixir.

Keeping the Jade Rabbit company in the Moon Palace is an immortal by the name of Wu Gang. This unfortunate being had been exiled by the Jade Emperor (the supreme deity in the Daoist cosmology) with the stipulation that amnesty could be extended only when he had succeeded in felling the cassia tree. Yet each time Wu Gang struck with his axe, the tree healed the cut immediately, dooming him to eternal futility. Among the Chinese people, perhaps the most popular of all the tales connected with Mid-Autumn Festival is that of Chang E, the Moon Lady, who turned into a three-legged toad when she ascended to the moon. Like the story of the rabbit, this one also originated in India. From the earliest times the various elements of this myth have been interwoven: the moon, the female essence (*yin*), water, and amphibians (the toad). This tale, then, is told and retold at Mid-Autumn Festival.

Chang E and her husband Hou Yi, the miraculous archer, lived during the reign of the legendary Emperor Yao (about 2000 B.C.). Hou Yi, who wielded a magic bow and shot magic arrows, was a most capable member of the Imperial

Guard. One day ten suns appeared in the sky. People on earth could not stand the heat and drought which continued for years on end. The emperor called Hou Yi before him and ordered him to shoot the extra suns out of the sky to succour the populace. Bringing all his skill to bear, Hou Yi knocked nine of them down leaving only the one.

After this Hou Yi's fame spread even to the Queen Mother of the West (Xi Wang Mu) in the far-off Kunlun Mountains. She summoned him to her fairy palace to reward him with the pill of immortality, first warning him: "You must not eat the pill immediately. First prepare yourself through praying and fasting for 12 months." Being a careful man, he took her advice to heart and set about his preparations, first hiding the pill in his house. Unfortunately, he was called away suddenly on an urgent mission. In his absence, his wife Chang E noticed a soft light and sweet odour emanating from a corner of the room. Taking the pill in her hand, she just could not refrain from taking a taste. The moment she swallowed it the law of gravity lost its power over her — she could fly! Not too long afterwards she heard her husband returning and flew in terror out of the window. Bow and arrow in hand, Hou Yi pursued her across half the sky, but a strong wind drove him back. Chang E flew all the way to the moon, but when she arrived, she was panting so hard from her exertions that she spat out the pill casing, which turned instantly into a jade rabbit. She herself became a three-legged toad. Ever since she has lived on the moon and continued to ward off the magic arrows shot by Hou Yi. Her husband built himself a palace on the sun and they see each other on the 15th of every month. Chang E and Hou Yi, symbolizing respectively the sun and the moon, have come to be regarded as embodying *yin* and *yang*, the negative and positive, dark and light, feminine and masculine duality which governs the universe.

Sacrifices to the Moon, and Moon Cakes

Moon cakes come on sale shortly before festival time. In the past, one could get some cakes shaped like pagodas, others like a horse and rider, fish or animals. Still others were decorated with the images of rabbits, flowers, or goddesses. There were a myriad different fillings available: sugar, melon seeds, almonds, orange peel, sweetened cassia blossom, or bits of ham and preserved beef. The cakes are of the northern and southern styles, but the latter (also called Guangdong-style) are the most popular and are available throughout the country.

Before 1949, toy shops also offered a large variety of toys to mark the occasion. One could also buy pictures of the moon palace or the Moon Goddess, Chang E, or of the rabbit sitting under the cassia tree mixing ingredients for the jade elixir.

Well-to-do people exchanged presents, mostly pears, grapes, pomegranates and moon cakes. The round shape of these objects symbolized not only the moon but also the unity of the family. On the evening before the Mid-Autumn Festival, friends would gather together for a sociable hour, eating cakes, drinking tea or sipping wine.

The following evening, offerings to the moon would be placed out in the open on an altar decorated with a picture of the Moon Palace or Moon Rabbit and perhaps a small clay figure of the rabbit. Because the moon is uniquely associated with *yin*, the feminine force, this whole ceremony was conducted by women. According to an old proverb, "Men do not worship the moon and women do not sacrifice to the Kitchen God." When the clouds dispersed and the moon rose, the ceremony began. The offerings, which were laid out on five platters, consisted of as many different kinds of fruit: apples, peaches, pomegranates (symbol of fertility), grapes and melons. Then would be brought forward the moon cakes, 13 in all — the number 13 symbolizing the number of months in a full lunar year. After that wine cups were filled, incense lit, and spirit money sent up in flames. Frequently there would also be offerings of beans or beanpods for the moon rabbit who was said to be particularly fond of these things. All the women in the family, one after another, stepped forward to kowtow. The sacrifices to the moon, which often lasted as late as midnight, concluded with the burning of the moon pictures.

Some Historical Notes

Moon cakes, a favoured delicacy among Chinese young and old, have also played an important role on at least one occasion in the drama of the overthrow of a dynasty. The following story relates how this came to be.

The Mongols overthrew the Song dynasty in 1279 and founded the Yuan dynasty with Kublai Khan, grandson of Genghis Khan as its first emperor. The last Song emperor was sent into captivity in Mongolia, but the crown prince succeeded in escaping. The Mongols proceeded to divide the entire population into four categories: they themselves made up the first category, the second included central Asian peoples who had earlier capitulated to their rule, the third consisted of the subjugated Hans in north China as well as the Nüzhen (Nuchen), Gaoli (Korean) and Qidan (Khitan) nationalities, and to the fourth category belonged all southern peoples, including the Han and other minority nationalities. The Mongol rulers treated the Han, especially those in the south, as slaves, to the extent that there was even open traffic in slaves, as if they were animals. Fertile crop land was turned into pasturage. Only Mongols or those of the second category were permitted to hold senior official posts. The Hans were forbidden to go out at night or to have lights in their houses, and no civilian was allowed to possess arms. Even the monasteries were forbidden to use objects of iron for religious purposes. To facilitate surveillance, the Mongol rulers did not permit the northern Han to live in the same villages with Mongols, while in the south all residents were organized into a system under which 20 households constituted a *jia*, of which the chief was a Mongol. The *jia* chiefs exercised absolute authority over the Han people under their rule and were cruel and unjust. The laws of the Yuan dynasty provided that if a Mongol killed a Han he might either be conscripted into the military or have to pay the victim's burial expenses. Han and other southerners were not allowed to defend themselves from attack; their only recourse was to appeal to officialdom. On the other hand, a Han who beat or killed a Mongol would be subjected to severe punishment. If a person from the fourth category were convicted of theft, he would have a tattoo imprinted on the face. Mongols and those of the second category guilty of the same crime were immune from this form of punishment.

Rebellions against the Mongols' brutal rule began in the

year 1351, the 11th year of the reign of Shun Di, the last emperor of the Yuan dynasty. The White Lotus secret society instigated a rebellion in Yingzhou and managed to occupy several districts. Their forces quickly grew to number 100,000 men. Encouraged by their example, the population in various other districts followed suit. Zhu Yuanzhang, who later became the founding emperor of the Ming dynasty in 1368, was at that time a low-ranking officer in the rebel army of Guo Zixing, but by 1353 he had become leader of a division several thousand strong. Having successfully taken the Dingyuan district in Anhui Province, he attacked Chuzhou Prefecture. The city was only lightly-defended, and the rebels were again successful.

The popular account of how the fall of Chuzhou occurred, however, is much more picturesque, whether or not it is actually true.

According to this version, the Jade Emperor in a rage had sent five gods to Chuzhou to afflict the people with plague. But one of the immortals (of the Daoist pantheon) was moved to compassion and sent one of his disciples to protect the people. This disciple was none other than Liu Bowen, Zhu Yuanzhang's senior counsellor. Arriving in the city, he held Daoist rites for three days and nights, reciting a complicated succession of incantations. Then he informed the populace that he had implored the five gods to spare the city, but that each family should nonetheless raise a flag at midnight on the 15th day of the month. They should also light lanterns and beat drums and gongs; only thus could they be saved from the pestilence. Liu Bowen then distributed moon cakes to all families in the city, telling each person that the cakes contained a slip of paper on which was written an incantation. If they took the appropriate action at the midnight hour, they would surely be saved. Liu then hastened away to return to his army.

The Mid-Autumn Festival came a few days later. After the usual festival activities had been completed, midnight struck and the whole city lit up the lanterns, raised flags, and beat drums and gongs. Breaking open their moon cakes, they all found slips of paper bearing the message: "Kill the Dazi (Tartars)". The people armed themselves with kitchen knives and wooden sticks, and just at that moment, Zhu Yuanzhang's army, which had stealthily approached the city, filled the air with deafening battle cries, beat on their drums and gongs, and lit a multitude of torches. The Yuan defenders had no idea of the strength or numbers of their attackers; they saw only the brightly burning lanterns, the fluttering flags, and heard the wild beating of drums and gongs. They fled in fear and confusion. Those who lingered were killed or made prisoners.

That, then, was how Zhu Yuanzhang is supposed to have captured the city. (The fact that Liu Bowen did not in actuality come over to Zhu Yuanzhang until 1359, six years after the attack on Chuzhou, clearly indicates that the above story is not entirely true. Liu was not a disciple of an immortal but rather a noted man of letters, a candidate who had passed the imperial examination and held the post of a junior district official in the Yuan dynasty.) Many centuries later moon cakes once again reappeared in a political role: around the time of the 1900 Boxer Rebellion, messages saying "Kill the foreigners" were sometimes placed in the cakes as a reaction against exploitation by the foreign powers.

The Mid-Autumn Festival Today

The tales concerning the moon rabbit and the story of Chang E are just as popular among people as ever, but now they are generally regarded merely as fairly tales. As far as I know, people no longer make offerings to the moon, as not many people still follow the old beliefs. One cannot find moon pictures, but artistic scrolls depicting Chang E with the rabbit in the Moon Palace can be bought all the year round. These tales have also been taken as themes for children's picture stories and dance dramas.

The Moon Festival today is an ordinary workday, basically a welcome opportunity to sit outside, weather permitting, and enjoy some time with friends and relatives, to watch the full moon and eat moon cakes.

The Kitchen God

Amidst the clamour of preparations for the Lunar New Year, time passed quickly until the 23rd day of the 12th lunar month (in the north) or the 24th (in the south), when the time came to make offerings to the Kitchen God (Zao Wang Ye). It was widely believed that the Kitchen God ascended to heaven on one of these two days to make his annual report on the behaviour of the members of each household.

In old China the Kitchen God commanded very high prestige among the people. In ancient times he was worshipped as the inventor of fire. When, much later, a special god of fire appeared in the Chinese pantheon, he was worshipped as a family god and the protector of the hearth.

The degree of respect accorded the Kitchen God was unusual in that people used to burn incense and candles before his shrine on the first and 15th days of each month, rather than on one festival only during the year, as was the case with most other gods. In addition all the cooks in Beijing would go to the Temple of the Kitchen God to honour their patron on the third day of the eighth lunar month, which was said to be his birthday.

Each household had a shrine for the Kitchen God in a corner on the back wall behind the hearth. It was usually blackened with smoke and frequently filled with cockroaches, which were referred to as "the horses of the god". These shrines could be made out of a variety of materials, including bamboo, wood and paper. Inside each one was pasted a picture of the Kitchen God in one of several forms. He was sometimes portrayed in a sitting position beside a fully harnessed horse, sometimes as a young man with a recording tablet in hand on which he wrote the things that he must report to heaven and sometimes as an old man seated next to his aged wife. Those families that were too poor to buy such paintings, would paste a small square of red paper on the god's shrine instead. Written on the paper were the name of the god, his title, and a special apology from the family, as follows:

> Oh, Kitchen God, oh, Kitchen God,
> Here are a bowl of water and three incense sticks.
> Our life this past year was not so good,
> Perhaps next year we'll offer you Manchurian sugar!

The Origin of the Kitchen God

The worship of the Kitchen God dates back over 2,000 years. *The Rites of Zhou*, a book of the Confucian school that records the decrees and regulations of both the Western Zhou dynasty (1066-770 B.C.) and the Warring States period (476-221 B.C.), states: "Zhu Rong, the son of Zhuan Xu and grandson of the Yellow Emperor, had been in charge of fire in life and was ordained God of the Kitchen after death. During the Zhou period, wealthy families placed oblations for him on their hearths." The philosophical book of Daoism *Huai Nan Zi*, which was completed during the Western Han dynasty (206 B.C.-25 A.D.), contains the following passage: "The Yellow Emperor invented the hearth and was worshipped as the Kitchen God

The Kitchen God

after his death." The Kitchen God is thus placed on the same footing as the Yellow Emperor who is considered to be the common ancestor of the Chinese people. The actual identity of the Kitchen God has been the subject of numerous interpretations over the course of time. The *Youyang Miscellanies*, a Tang dynasty (618-907 A.D.) book which describes everyday life and social customs of the time, claims that the family name of the Kitchen God is Zhang. Owing perhaps to the fact that the older women did most of the cooking, people at one time believed that the Kitchen God was an old woman. Later on the belief that the god was a young lady became prevalent. Finally the most widely accepted version was that it was a young man named Zhang Sheng, about whom there is a widely circulated tale. Zhang Sheng had a large estate and much livestock. His wife Guo Dingxiang was virtuous and beautiful. The couple got along extremely well until he took a lazy and malicious concubine named Li Haitang. Before much time had passed Li succeeded in persuading Zhang to divorce his first wife. Without her supervision, Zhang and Li squandered his wealth away within two years. Then the concubine walked out on him and married someone else, while Zhang was reduced to begging. Weak from hunger, he passed out at the gate of a household one bitterly cold winter day. A maid from the house discovered him and helped him into their kitchen, where she gave him something to eat. On asking about the mistress, Zhang learned that not only was she a virtuous lady who took pleasure in helping others, especially the aged and poor, but that she was also single. This aroused in him a feeling of deep admiration. When he saw the good lady coming toward him through the window, however, he realized that she was none other than his first wife Guo

Dingxiang. Overcome with shame, he dared not face her. But where to hide? The hearth was the only possible place, so he crawled into the hearth and was burned to death. Discovering that her ex-husband had been burned to ashes, Guo was filled with both pity and sadness. She died not long after this tragedy occurred. When the Jade Emperor learned of the story, he praised Zhang Sheng for his courage in admitting his mistakes and declared him to be the Kitchen God. Later the common people worshipped his first wife as a deity as well.

The worship of the Kitchen God has a very long history. The great Han dynasty emperor Wu Di personally officiated at ceremonies in the god's honour. China's Kitchen God functioned as a judge of the family's morality, just as did the Fire God of the Hindu religion. Both the Hindu Fire God and the Chinese Kitchen God mediated between the human world and that of the gods. The Kitchen God's manner of coming and going (the burning of his portrait sends him to the heavens) may have originated from the natural phenomenon of lightning, which was superstitiously believed to be the means by which God sent fire to earth.

The Kitchen God was so deeply rooted in the Chinese people's hearts that both Daoism and Buddhism adopted the concept so as to facilitate their own expansion. Thus Daoist mythology evolved a Kitchen God with a number of different titles fitting into its own rather complex pantheon. The Buddhists argued that their Kitchen God was fundamentally different from the Daoists' in that theirs was a celestial being who became a Buddhist monk during the Tang dynasty and who, after his death, was chosen to preside over the vegeterian diet of the monks. This is of course an obvious rationalization of the Buddhist accommodation with Chinese popular beliefs.

Worship of the Kitchen God

As mentioned earlier, the Chinese believed that on the 23rd or 24th day of the 12th month the Kitchen God made his annual report to the Jade Emperor on the conduct and attitudes of each member of the household. For this occasion, people placed offerings before his portrait and pasted around it three inscriptions, a horizontal one above and a vertical one on each side. Frequently the horizontal one would read: "The Lord Kitchen God". The two vertical ones might say "Speak Well (of us) in Heaven", and "Bring Good Fortune (to us) on Earth". Because the Kitchen God represented the sovereign of a household, the ceremony was presided over by the head of the family. Therefore, the custom in many areas was to exclude females, even the mistress of the household. Local customs varied from place to place, however. An elderly lady from Anhui Province told me that in her hometown only old people (male or female) were allowed to participate. During the Tang dynasty the offerings were reported as consisting of a cup of tea and three incense sticks. Before 1949, peasants usually offered light snacks made from malt sugar and glutinous rice flour for the occasion. But wealthy families would be more extravagant, of course; water melon, cakes, preserved fruits, meat, fresh oranges, and other foods might be given to the Kitchen God. In some areas people smeared the god's lips with honey so that he would say only sweet things in heaven, and it was said that some people even used opium to make him sleepy and forgetful of all unpleasant incidents. Using the same sort of logic, rice wine might be splashed on the painting. We can see that these offerings had practically become a means of bribery. Nevertheless, the general opinion held that people through their exertions on the god's behalf, could ensure his cooperation in obtaining the blessings and protection of heaven in the coming year.

The Kitchen God's shrine was carried out into the courtyard, and the food, liquor and tea were placed before it. As the pungent scent of the burning incense wafted toward the heavens, the head of the family offered prayers on his family's behalf and kowtowed before the shrine. The deafening roar of exploding firecrackers then brought the ceremony to a satisfactory close. In old China firecrackers accompanied virtually every important ritual because of people's sincere belief that the noise of firecrackers brings pleasure and comfort to both gods and men and strikes fear into the hearts of all evil spirits. Usually it was the youngsters who set off the firecrackers, this being a part of the ceremony in which they could actively participate. Finally the assembled family members burned the god's portrait together with some spirit money (for his expenses along the way), and the Kitchen God ascended to heaven amid the flame and smoke. Neither was his steed to be neglected: people in some areas threw straw and beanstalks into the flames as fodder and tea or water was sprinkled on the ground to slake the horse's thirst. Simultaneously a few people would throw beans or peas onto the building's tile rooftop to imitate the sound of ascending footsteps and hoofbeats.

After the departure of the heavenly inspector, people could finally relax for a few days. They were released from some of the prohibitions that normally applied to the women particularly while working in the kitchen; now they were permitted to comb their hair, wash their hands, and sharpen their knives in front of the Kitchen God's shrine and even spit toward the hearth.

Chu Xi, the Lunar New Year's Eve

Chu Xi is the romanization of the two Chinese characters which together mean New Year's Eve; literally, to get rid of (*Chu*) the last evening (*Xi*) of the passing year. Traditionally this evening was a very important time in the Spring Festival celebrations. The entire compound of a typical household blazed with lights, inside as well as outside the house. The implied symbolism here involved driving bad luck and evil spirits away from all corners of the family compound, on the one hand, and the welcoming of the coming bright future, on the other. Supper on New Year's Eve was a great feast to be enjoyed by the whole family. Later they would pass the evening playing cards, throwing dice, and in other games. This ritual had a double meaning: one was to see off the passing year, known in Chinese as *Ci Sui*, and the other was to usher in the new year, or *Shou Sui* in Chinese. Peasants in certain areas went outside at 1 a.m. to beat the dunghills (kept for fertilizer) with sticks. This rather strange custom was their way of asking for happiness and wealth in the forthcoming year. In some other areas, people placed their shoes with soles upward when they went to bed in the belief that any bad luck of misfortune brought by the evil spirits would fall onto the soles. The next morning one had only to walk a few steps in one's shoes and the evil spirits' scheme would be thwarted.

Of all the rituals associated with Spring Festival, the most important were the triple rites: the offering to the ancestors, the offering to earth and heaven and the offering to the God of Wealth. Because of the tremendous regional distinctions that have always existed in China, as well as class differences and even professional distinctions, one cannot with any degree of confidence describe "the" correct manner of performing the triple rites. This book concentrates on the practices obtaining in Beijing. Some families repeated each one twice, once shortly before midnight and once in the early hours of the morning. Most families held them only once each, however. All were presided over by the head of the family.

Prior to the ceremonies, pine branches and sesame twigs were spread over the courtyard. The sound of the wind blowing through them was taken as the approaching footsteps of an evil spirit and the signal for vigilance. All the doors leading into the compound from the outside were shut and sealed with two paper strips which had to remain absolutely intact until the next morning. Any knock at the door during the night would not be answered for fear that some wandering ghost might be trying to enter.

The Offering to the Ancestors

The significance of this ceremony was, in the first place, a gesture of remembrance and respect toward the ancestors and, secondly, a formal means of giving thanks for past favours and requesting continued protection for their descendants.

As soon as dusk fell, meat, vegetables and fruits were placed in front of the ancestral tablet and incense sticks, candles and spirit money burnt. Then, amidst the explosions of firecrackers, the head of the family would kneel down and bow deeply before the tablet. If he were away, either his wife or eldest son would substitute for him. People also sometimes threw salt into the fire. The crackling sound thus produced was considered to be auspicious. Then came the New Year greetings of the younger generations to their elders. All the younger members of the family, sons, daughters-in-law, and other unmarried children, knelt before members of the senior generations and knocked their heads on the ground three times (the ritual kowtow) to wish them happiness in the New Year.

At midnight people would often change into their New Year clothes. Each youngster received as a New Year gift some money wrapped in a piece of red paper, which signified that the recipient would have a happy New Year and never want for money.

The Offering to Heaven and Earth

The purpose of this ceremony was to ensure favourable weather and a bumper harvest in the coming year. A book published in 1868 had the following description: "This ceremony is carried out the first thing in the morning on New Year's Day, actually beginning at four or five o'clock. Most adults do not sleep the entire night. The altar table is usually placed in advance in the front part of the main hall. Placed on the table are an earthern rice steamer filled with rice, five or ten bowls of various dishes, ten cups of tea, ten cups filled with wine, two red candles, and three incense sticks, or, alternatively, a piece of sandalwood. Two pine boughs or some flowers are placed in the rice steamer. One also can find on the table ten pairs of chopsticks, on top of which are two pieces of paper tinsel, one standing for gold and another standing for silver. Such paper tinsel is used only on special occasions like the Lunar New Year. On top of the two pieces of tinsel are two piles of spirit money. A new almanac dangles from a red thread tied to one of the chopsticks. Five kinds of dried fruit are placed under the paper tinsel and on top of the rice. Last of all, oranges are put on a platter or basin in the middle of the table. As soon as all the preparations are finished, firecrackers are set off on the street in front of the house or at the compound gate. Now the male head of the family, incense sticks in hand, kneels before the altar table and touches his head on the ground three times. Then he stands up and places the incense sticks into an incense burner on the altar. By this ceremony the family pay their respects to heaven and earth as well as express their appreciation and gratitude for past blessings. In the end firecrackers are once again exploded and the spirit money burnt. All the offerings on the altar usually remain intact for one or two days."

The above is a description of the offering to heaven and earth as it would have been practised among wealthy families. In the north barley or millet would have taken the place of the rice.

The Offering to the God of Wealth

In China the worship of the household gods, one of whom is the God of Wealth, preceded the appearance of both Buddhism and Daoism. The precise identity of the God of Wealth is unclear. Though sharing the same title, the God of Wealth in succeeding ages may not actually have been the same deity. He was most often portrayed as an armoured general riding a black tiger and carrying a whip. In the *Roster of Enfeoffed Spirits* written in the Ming dynasty, he is said to be a marshal, and under Emperor Zhou of the Shang dynasty (1600-1100 B.C.) a wizard named Zhao Gongming.

People made offerings not only to the auspicious gods such as those of wealth, happiness and the kitchen, but also to evil ones like the five gods of plague. The purpose of the latter category of offerings was to persuade these gods not to visit one's home, thus sparing oneself hopefully from misfortune and disaster.

The God of Wealth was invited to return home on the fourth day of the Lunar New Year in some provinces and on New Year's Day in Beijing. Like that of the Kitchen God, the portrait of the God of Wealth could be found hanging in virtually every household, and just as the Kitchen God's portrait was renewed annually, so also was the God of Wealth's.

Lu Xun gave the following description of the atmosphere in his home on New Year's Eve when he was a child: "Beyond any question the happiest time of the year was *Chu Xi*. After bidding farewell to the past year (*Ci Sui*), I put my New Year's gift — some money wrapped in a piece of red paper — beside my pillow. Tomorrow it would be entirely at my own option as to how to spend it. Then Ah Chang would come in and put an 'orange of luck' on my bedside. 'Remember, my dear,' she said very seriously, 'tomorrow is New Year's Day. Say "Happy New Year" the first thing when you see me tomorrow. Can you remember this? You must remember it, for it will have an important effect on how my next year goes. You mustn't say anything else before this. Afterwards I'll give you a section of the "orange of luck".' She then would pick up the orange again and wave it before my eyes. 'It will assure you of the fulfillment of all your wishes in the New Year.' "

In his novel *The New Year's Celebration*, he wrote: "If I remember correctly, New Year's Eve indeed brought about a festive air in both country and city. You could almost feel the approaching of the New Year in the air. Rays of light came out occasionally from behind the usually heavy, dark clouds. The joyful sound of firecrackers which accompanied the heaven-ascending God of Wealth permeated the atmosphere. The nearer one stood to the firecrackers, the louder was the sound in one's ears. Before the whole string was finished, the air was full of the smell of gun-powder.

"All in the family took an active part in the preparation of the offerings for the various ceremonies in order to demonstrate their piety and devotedness to the gods and obtain more blessings from them in the new year. For this occasion, chickens and ducks had been slaughtered and pork bought. The womenfolk found no end of work. As a result of steeping in cold water for too long, their silver-braceleted hands become red and swollen. When all the dishes were prepared, they were placed on the candle-lit altar table together with several pairs of chopsticks. This was how the offerings were made. Only the male members of the family, however, could participate in the actual ceremony. Humbly and reverently, they prayed to the gods and invited them to partake of the offerings. On the completion of the ceremonies, more firecrackers were set off. Such ceremonies were repeated every year in every household, assuming, of course, that they could afford the necessary food, candles and firecrackers."

The Spring Festival (New Year's Day)

Since early morning all the gates were closed and the shops shuttered. In the place of the usual bustling activity, one found only silence and the wrappers of exploded firecrackers lying on all the doorsteps. Throughout the day, the people of this industrious nation relaxed and amused themselves with recreational activities, either indoors or out, such as playing dice, cards and above all, mah-jong. The day was also the occasion for paying New Year calls on friends and relatives to exchange greetings and wish one another the happiest possible new year. While children received the small red packets of money, as described earlier, adults were treated to tea, cigarettes, peanuts, melon-seeds and sweets.

In the old days wealthy households used to celebrate every day for the first two weeks of the new year. Though not able to afford such extended celebrations, the poor could still have up to four weeks of vacation from work.

Afterword

On the basis of the previous chapters one can see the tendency for the original significance or content of the traditional festivals to weaken and the customs and habits handed down from the old days to decline. In recent years, however, the historical background of such festivals has been taught to children in the schools.

The new holidays, such as International Labour Day, Women's Day, and Children's Day, are given increased importance. Working women take half a day off on March 8; school children have a vacation from class work on June 1; all working people celebrate Labour Day (May 1) with a day off. On these holidays, many cultural activities of all kinds are conducted, including dramatic performances, films, and special television programmes. Newspapers publish articles and radio stations present specials to mark the occasion. Thus, these new festivals are given official recognition and increased attention as compared to the traditional festivals, with the exception of the Spring Festival, which remains officially sanctioned. These changes will inevitably affect the attitudes prevailing among the people, especially the younger generation.

There can be occasions on which traditional festivals become linked with current political issues. On *Qing Ming* (Pure Brightness) Festival in 1976, for instance, huge crowds of people gathered in front of the Monument to the Revolutionary Martyrs in Beijing's Tian'anmen Square to place wreaths and offer memorials to Zhou Enlai. These spontaneous activities in the late Premier's honour turned into an open manifestation of resistance to the Gang of Four prior to their downfall.

Appendix:
Festivals of the Chinese Minority Nationalities

The Zhuang (Chuang) Song Festival

The Song Festival (*Ge Xu*) is a literal translation of the Han name for this gala occasion. More informative, the original Zhuang name actually means "songs for singing in the fields".

As the name suggests, songs, mostly in the form of chorus and antiphony, dominate the three days of revelries. Participants usually improvise as they go along. Similar to Han folksongs, Zhuang songs are largely five- or seven-character quatrains.

The occasion takes place on the third day of the third moon in the Chinese traditional calendar among the Zhuang communities in Guangxi Zhuang Autonomous Region.

The Bai (Pai) Third Moon Fair

This is more an annual bazaar than a festival. Its origin can be traced back to the early years of the Tang dynasty (618-907) when it was no more than a small market at Dali, modern capital of the Bai Autonomous Prefecture in Yunnan Province. In the course of time, however, it has gradually grown to its present size and offers a great variety of goods for the visitors. There are traditional style decorations as well as marble and embroidery articles made by the Bai people. The festival also provides an opportunity for fun with dramas, dancing, horse racing, ball and chess games, etc.

Now the occasion has become a multi-national gathering with Huis, Tibetans, Yis, Dais (Tais), Naxis (Nahsis) and Hans as well as Bais. It takes place from the 15th to the 20th day in the third moon of the Chinese traditional calendar.

The Dai (Tai) Water-Sprinkling Festival

In the Dai calendar this annual carnival is the counterpart of the Han New Year.

Celebrated as the end of the old year, the first of the three days of festivities is marked by such ceremonies as washing Buddhist images in the hope of a bumper harvest and such games as dragon boat racing. The third and last day, known as the Prince of All Days, is New Year's Day. Chief among the day's activities are "rocket-launching" and "pouch-flying". The former is supposed to bring luck to whoever gets one of the five amulets contained in the bamboo rocket. The latter is mainly a way for Dai girls to choose their boy-friends. Each girl throws a pouch at the youth she has set her heart on. The carnival reaches its climax on the second day. When the water-sprinkling spree begins water is splashed over everyone, including strangers, as a symbol of blessing and honour.

The Tibetan New Year

China's Tibetans have a lunar-solar calendar of their own.

Their New Year's Day, therefore, falls on a different date from that of the Hans. Even among Tibetans themselves the date varies from place to place, falling on the first day of the tenth moon in some areas, the first day of the eleventh moon in some others and the first day of the first moon in still others. But one thing is in common: they start preparing for their New Year almost a month earlier by making purchases necessary for the coming celebration.

Offerings are made to gods and historical figures on New Year's Eve and repeatedly throughout the whole occasion in the hope of a good harvest.

Another important feature of this occasion is the *hada* ribbon, a long strip of silk, usually white, which is presented to guests. The longer the ribbon, the greater honour it signifies.

The Mongolian Nadam Fair

"Nadam" in the Mongolian language means "recreation" or "games". But this is not all there is to the modern Nadam Fair. Besides the traditional horse racing, archery and wrestling, there are variety shows, films, exhibitions and sports competitions as well as a lot of business activity.

Of all these, wrestling is perhaps the most popular with Mongolians. It is said to have been included among the three martial skills (the other two being horsemanship and archery) by Genghis Khan (reigned 1206-1227). In subsequent centuries it gradually became so popular that great wrestlers were, and still are, generally admired by the Mongolian people.

The Yao Danu Festival

Danu Festival is a major celebration of the Yao people. It takes place at irregular intervals of one, three or 12 years, depending on local traditions and the year's harvest.

Otherwise known as Ancestress Festival, it is held in honour of Miluotuo, the legendary earliest ancestress of the Yao. The festival celebration is largely in the form of a gathering. For three to five successive days, Yaos talk and picnic while enjoying a great variety of performances, including dances, local songs, martial arts and *suona* (a wood-wind instrument) music, as well as participating in hide-and-seek games.

Besides these, special mention should be made of the brass drum dance, performed by a woman and two men one of whom beats the drum to keep time. It is perhaps the most important event during the festival.

The festival falls on the 29th day of the fifth moon in the traditional Chinese lunar calendar.

The Yi Torch Festival

The Torch Festival is celebrated on the 24th day of the sixth moon in the Chinese lunar calendar. A major occasion with Yis, it may last from one to three days.

During the daytime Yis go on a joyous drinking spree while watching wrestling, bullfighting, archery and horse racing. But it is not until night comes that the climax of festivities is reached. In the darkness hundreds of torches dance about weaving ephemeral patterns. The most fun perhaps is derived from the so-called "splashing fire". One participant will reach his torch over toward another while sprinkling a handful of inflammable material over the flames, raising a spray of sparks which dance around his opponent, who will then joyfully take his "revenge".

The Miao New Year Festival

Like Tibetans, the Miao communities in Guizhou and Guangxi provinces have a traditional New Year Festival of their own. It comes either in the ninth, tenth or eleventh moon of the Chinese lunar calendar and may last as long as 13 days.

The occasion is traditionally marked by bullfighting and, especially, by the *lusheng* dance. The latter in its variety of forms is actually a group dance involving as many as a hundred *lusheng* (a reed-pipe wind instrument) of different sizes, the longest being about six metres.

This is also an opportunity for courtship among the young. There is usually a place in every Miao village specially staked off, in which boys and girls meet and fall in love through an exchange of songs.

The Dong (Tung) Rocket Festival

The Rocket Festival (*Hua Pao Jie*) is a major occasion in Dong life. It is said to have its origin back in the Qing dynasty (1644-1911), when rockets were employed by businessmen to attract customers. But in due course it lost its commercial significance and became a pure gala occasion.

On the chosen day the rocket launcher is first paraded

through streets and then, amid a burst of gunshots, three iron rings, representing Victory, Unity and Happiness, are fired into the sky.

Following this climax the funfair begins and in the evening dramas and film shows provide entertainment for all.

Though this is a common time for festivities among the Dong communities, there is no fixed date generally accepted.

The Bouyei (Puyi) Dancing Party

The Dancing Party (*Tiao Hua Hui*) is a traditional occasion in Bouyei's festive life. During the 20 days of the festival there are usually local dramas and a lot of merrymaking and courting.

The young usually take part in singing and dancing together. Some of the courting couples, however, prefer the quiet of the riverside where they play music to each other.

Bouyei dramas usually tell of heroes who overcome fiends to ensure a good harvest.

The festival lasts from the first to the 21st day of the first moon in the Chinese traditional lunar calendar. On the 22nd day, known as "bring home the sheep", the girl goes to her boy-friend's home.

"Flower" or "Youngster" Songfest

"Flower" or "Youngster" are both local names for a kind of folksong popular in the northwestern part of China. The songfest is held by quite a few minority nationality communities. Participants, sometimes in rival groups, usually improvise as they exchange songs. As is the case with most Chinese folksongs, love and historical events are two of the main themes.

The five-day songfest begins on the sixth day of the sixth moon in the traditional Chinese lunar calendar; participants include Tujias (Tuchia), Huis, Dongxiangs, Salas and Baoans.

The Corban in China

The Corban is one of the major festivals in China's Moslem life. It was introduced to China in the seventh century as part of Islam, which is now practised by about one-fourth of China's minority nationality population — 15 million people, including Huis, Uygurs, Kazaks, Usbeks, Tajiks, Salas, Dongxiangs and Baoans.

An important event, it begins with a house-cleaning before the festival and continues with bathing and worshipping to mark the occasion. If it is financially possible, animals such as sheep, cows and camels are slaughtered and presented to guests. Many people gather at the mosque and exchange greetings. In public places young people dance to music until night falls.

The Corban takes place on the tenth day of the tenth moon in the Moslem calendar.

The Jing (Ching) Singing Festival

The Singing Festival (*Ha Jie*) is an annual tradition with Jings. Chief among its variety of activities is singing, as the name suggests. There is a traditional repertoire of songs specially reserved for the occasion sung by a trio of singers, one male and two females. Most are songs of historical and legendary figures and love songs. As tradition demands, a finely-constructed wooden building called the Singing Hall (*Ha Ting*), is specially kept for this carnival.

The date of the festival varies from place to place and it usually lasts for a couple of days.

The Lisu Festival of the Scimitar Rungs

This is a traditional gala occasion among Lisus in Yunnan Province. The general focus during the festivities is on five men, who perform wonders to the horror and admiration of all. On the night of the first day four piles of fire will be lit on which the men dance barefoot while juggling burning embers in their hands, brushing them across their cheeks and doing somersaults. But it is not until the second day that the climax comes. The same quintet, again barefoot, will climb a ladder with 36 scimitars, blade upwards, forming its rungs. The secret to all this is *Qigong*, the Chinese breath-energy exercises.

The Jingpo (Chingpo) Dancing Festival (Mu Nao Zong Ge)

This is an occasion of revelry for the Jingpos, usually held in celebration of a good harvest. Before the carnival, a stage with an impressive backdrop of crossed scimitars is set up in the fields where the dancing will take place.

The mass dance usually begins at sunrise, following the entertainment of visitors with food and fruits. At the height of the festival thousands of people may be seen dancing to the music until night falls.